INTO GEOGRAPHY

3 The Geography of the Environment

Patricia Harrison · Steve Harrison
Mike Pearson

Nelson

Acknowledgements

American Arts, Dept. of English, Exeter University
Fred Coupe
Jane Demers, USA
Linda Edmondson
Heathrow Airport Ltd
Legal and General Assurance Society
Marks and Spencers
The Post Office
James Price
Radio Rentals
Hogg Robinson
St. George's Shopping Centre, Preston

Designed by Barrie Richardson

Illustrated by Terry Bambrook, Ray Mutimer, PFB Art and Type Ltd, Barrie Richardson and Colin Smithson.

Cover photograph by Ingleborough Hall Outdoor Education Centre

Photographs by courtesy of Barnaby's Picture Library (pp.39, 41), British Museum (Natural History) (p.54), Colin Greenway (p.53), Steve Harrison (p.33), National Coal Board (p.61), Legal and General Assurance Society (pp.4, 5, 6), Peter Newark's Western Americana (p.45), Elizabeth Pearson (p.39, 40), University of Washington Libraries (p.45).

Thomas Nelson and Sons Ltd
Nelson House   Mayfield Road
Walton-on-Thames   Surrey
KT12 5PL   UK

51 York Place
Edinburgh
EH1 3JD   UK

Thomas Nelson (Hong Kong) Ltd
Toppan Building 10/F
22A Westlands Road
Quarry Bay   Hong Kong

Thomas Nelson Australia
102 Dodds Street
South Melbourne
Victoria 3205
Australia

Nelson Canada
1120 Birchmount Road
Scarborough   Ontario
M1K 5G4   Canada

© Patricia Harrison, Steve Harrison, Mike Pearson 1986

First published by E J Arnold and Son Ltd 1976
ISBN 0-560-66713-2

This edition published by Thomas Nelson and Sons Ltd 1990
ISBN 0-17-410460-X
NPN 9 8 7 6 5 4 3 2

Printed in Hong Kong.

CONTENTS

ST. GEORGE'S CENTRE

"I know you're tired. It's a long walk to the butchers but then we'll go home"

1960

Look at this picture of Sally and David's grandma, Mrs Hudson. It shows her out shopping in 1960 when she was 32 years old. With her are Sally and David's mother and uncle aged 7 and 5 at the time.

Assignment A

Mrs Hudson did not have a car in 1960. She went shopping in town by bus.

1 List the difficulties Mrs Hudson faced shopping in 1960.

Think about: weather, time, distance, safety, transport.

2 Mrs Hudson went shopping every day. Can you suggest why?

Assignment B

Shopping became easier when the 'St. George's Centre' was opened in 1964. The picture below shows Mrs Hudson using the centre.

Compare the pictures of the shopping centre with the picture of shopping in 1960.

1 What dangers are no longer present?

2 Mrs Hudson now enjoys shopping. Why?

3 It takes her less time.

Can you suggest reasons?

4 In the top picture Mrs Hudson is soaking wet.

How has the situation changed in the shopping centre?

5 Try and imagine the centre on a cold icy day in January. Would it be safe for shoppers?

.1969.

fishergate walk

HARRY FE

TELEPHONE   REGAL   sale

It's hard work using these steps at my age. There's a new shopping centre in the next town. I'll go there next time!

·1979·

Assignment C

1 Look at the 2 photos taken before and after the alterations. List the changes you can see.

2 Copy and complete the chart by saying what advantages shoppers gained from the changes.

Changes	Advantages to shoppers
Centre covered by a roof	
Lift for the disabled	
Lift for prams	
More attractive decoration	
Heating	
Doors to entrances	
Music playing	
Escalators up and down	

3 List the changes in order of importance to
  a) Yourself
  b) A parent with a baby
  c) A senior citizen
  d) A disabled person in a wheelchair

4 An old man sat on the wooden bench every evening and scattered seed for the pigeons. How would he feel about the changes?

The owners of St. George's realised they needed to make changes or their customers would shop in other centres.

They thought carefully about what would make their centre attractive to shoppers.

The plan of the Lower Level of St. George's Centre shows the position of businesses in the precinct.

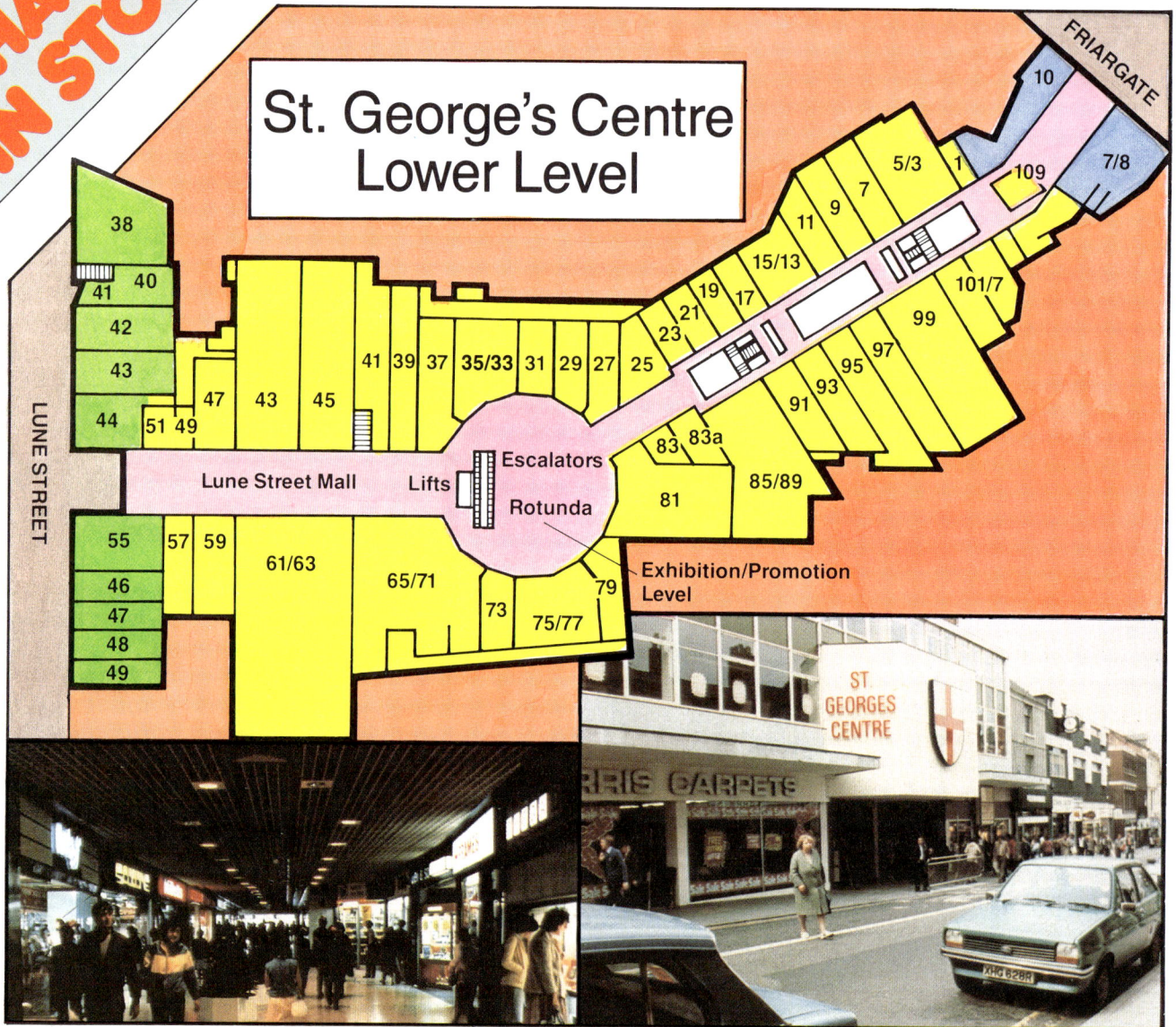

St. George's Centre Lower Level

Map labels: 38, 41, 40, 42, 43, 44, 51, 49, 47, 43, 45, 41, 39, 37, 35/33, 31, 29, 27, 25, 23, 21, 19, 17, 15/13, 11, 9, 7, 5/3, 1, 10, 109, 7/8, 101/7, 99, 97, 95, 93, 91, 85/89, 83, 83a, 81, 55, 57, 59, 61/63, 65/71, 73, 75/77, 79, 46, 47, 48, 49

LUNE STREET
FRIARGATE
Lune Street Mall — Lifts — Escalators — Rotunda
Exhibition/Promotion Level

Friargate Walk

1 Atherton Newsagent Tobacconist
3/5 United Chemists
7 Kenyons Coffee House Confectionery
9 Slaters Boys & Menswear
11 Prime Cut Butchery
13/15 Radio Rentals
17 Regal Textiles
19 Jean Jeannie
21 Hermit Wool
23 Walco Leather
25 Wheeldon's Butchery
27 Rumbelows
29 Hen House Farm Products
31 Ann Christian Fashions
33/35 Focus TV & Video
37 F & S Trading
39 —
41 The Larder Cafe Entrance to Precinct Restaurant
45 Superdrug
43 Cordon Bleu Freezer Food Centre
47 Eat Easy Restaurant
49 Zellers Jewellers
51 A.T. Mays, Travel
55 Stokers Carpets
57 Dollond & Aitchison Opticians
59 Peter Dominic, Off-Licence
61/63 Argos Catalogue Showroom
65/71 Mothercare
73 Carrade Cards
75/77 Carters Toys & Prams
79 D.B.I. Fashion
81 Gas Showroom
83 Twigy Fashions
83a Frasers Jewellers
85/89 Marks & Spencer
91 Stour Footwear
93 Moniques Fashions
95 Olivers Shoes
97 Supercards
99 Studio 4
101/7 Greenwoods The Mans Shop
109 Flower for you

Lune Street

38 Ladbrokes
40/41 Glacier Sport
42 Taylors Opticians Ltd
43 Barratts
43 Preston Business Venture
44 Britannia Building Society
46 Lindley Travel
47 Neil Price Menswear
48 Yorkshire Building Society
49 Singer Sewing Machine

Friargate

7/8 Harris Carpets
10 Harry Fenton

1 Mrs Hudson visited the Centre. She arrived at the Lune Street entrance and left through the Friargate exit. During her visit she went to the following units: 61, 81, 57, 47, 65, 85, 51, 73, 1, 11.

Work out a sensible route for Mrs Hudson.

2 a) List the shops she visited.   b) Write a shopping list to match her journey.

3 If unit 47 had been closed which unit could she have visited instead?

4 Copy and complete the chart below. Put a tick each time you identify a 'type' on the plan. For instance Unit 48, The Yorkshire Building Society, provides a financial service so a ✓ will go in that box. If you cannot identify a 'type' leave it out.

Department stores	Travel	Catering	Chemist Optician	Financial Services	Jewellers	Newsagent Stationery	Food and Drink shops	Footwear and clothes	Household Goods
				✓					

5 a) Which type of service occurs most often?
   b) Why do you think there are more food shops than opticians?

6 What month of the year will be the busiest for unit 75?

7 Choose 4 'types' of unit and list 5 items you could obtain from each.

Personal Research

1 Interview your grandparents about town centre shopping when they were young. Think about:

a) How did they travel?

b) What did goods cost when they were your age?

c) Which shops are popular now which were unknown forty years ago?

2 Town centre shops spend up to £100,000 on shop fronts and fittings. This picture shows an artist's impression of what a shop front will look like in the year 2,000.

Choose a different type of store and design your own shop front.

One step further

1 List the businesses in St. George's Centre which you can find in your local town centre.

2 Compare a shopping centre you know well with the St. George's Centre.

a) What features of the St. George's Centre would improve your local centre?

b) Are there any features which would be useful additions to the St: George's Centre?

WHERE TO SHOP

(Speech bubbles:)
- Have you settled in your new home?
- Just about. Where's the best place to shop?
- Well.. that depends on whether you have a car and what you want to buy!
- Yes we DO have a car.
- Well.. We DON'T and look here comes my husband now!
- GROAN
- Better make him a nice cup of tea!
- Come in! There are three shops to choose from.. I'll draw you a MAP!

Assignment A

1 Mrs Davidson and her family have just moved into the area. Do you think they have come from another part of the same town or from a completely different area? Explain your answer.

2 If her neighbour's husband has been shopping in the town centre how might he have travelled there?

3 How can this limit what he buys?

4 Will Mrs Davidson be able to buy more or less than her neighbour if she takes her car when she goes shopping?

Look at the map Mrs Davidson's neighbour drew for her. Pictures of the shopping areas have been added to help you.

We call shopping area **1** a 'Local Shopping Area', area **2** a 'Suburban Shopping Complex', and area **3** a 'City Centre'.

One step further A

List the advantages and disadvantages of going shopping:

a) by car   b) by bus
c) on foot   d) by taxi

Think about: parking, weather, cost, weight, speed, convenience.

Assignment B

Complete the chart.
Say which shopping area Mr and Mrs Davidson would visit for these purposes.

PURPOSE	AREA		
	1	2	3
Post a Letter	✓		
Visit the bank			
Buy stepladders			
Buy 2 weeks groceries			
Obtain cheap petrol			
Choose a new carpet			
Buy chips for lunch			
Buy plants for the garden			

One step further B

1 Make three separate shopping lists. One list for the local area, one for the suburban complex and one for the city centre.

2 Even if the local grocer sells beans some people will still buy them at supermarkets, why?

1 Interview your parents and four adults you know well. Find out how often they visit the different types of shopping area.

2 Talk to your grandparents or other older people you know well. Ask them about their shopping habits 25 years ago.

3 Compare these answers with the answers to question 1. How have shopping habits changed over the last 25 years?

Most people today live in **villages, towns** or **cities.** These are all names of **settlements** of different sizes. Nearly all settlements began as small villages. Some grew to be large towns or even cities, others remained small and are still called villages.

Imagine that you lived long ago. You are one of a group of farmers looking for a place to build your farms where you will keep animals and grow crops. You would want to choose the best site for your farm. Which of these two sites would you choose? Give your reasons.

The map on the opposite page shows an area of land without settlements. You must decide where you and your farming friends will build a settlement. Think carefully about these factors: You will need

- Clean water. Rivers are not always clean. A spring is better
- Building Materials
- Land suitable for grazing animals and for growing crops. The lower slopes of a hill are often suitable for grazing. Flat well-drained land is often suitable for crops and grazing
- Fuel
- A place where you can defend yourself if attacked
- Natural shelter from the rain and wind
- Your site should be easy to reach from your farming land, fuel and water
- Hunting and fishing are other ways of obtaining food

Assignment

1 Look at the following squares:
   How would you use what you find there?
   (F,8) (A,3) (E,7) (F,2) (E,5) (C,8) (D,9).

2 Choose the best grid square from those listed
   a) To shelter from the wind (A,8) (D,8) (E,5)
   b) To obtain clean water (D,1) (E,3) (C,5)
   c) For picking fruits and berries (A,6) (D,4)(F,8)
   d) For collecting roofing material (A,3) (D,4) (G,7).

One step further

Now you must choose which of the sites A B C D or E is the best location for your settlement.

1 Discuss the good points and bad points of each site with a friend.

2 Complete this chart, it will help you decide. The top line has been done for you.

	A	B	C	D	E
Clean water	✓	✗	✓	✗	✗
Grazing land					
Land for crops					
Shelter					
Building materials					
Fuel					
Defence					
Fishing					
Hunting					

3 Which site would you choose for your settlement?

4 If a second group of people settled in grid square (C,5), what problems would they face?

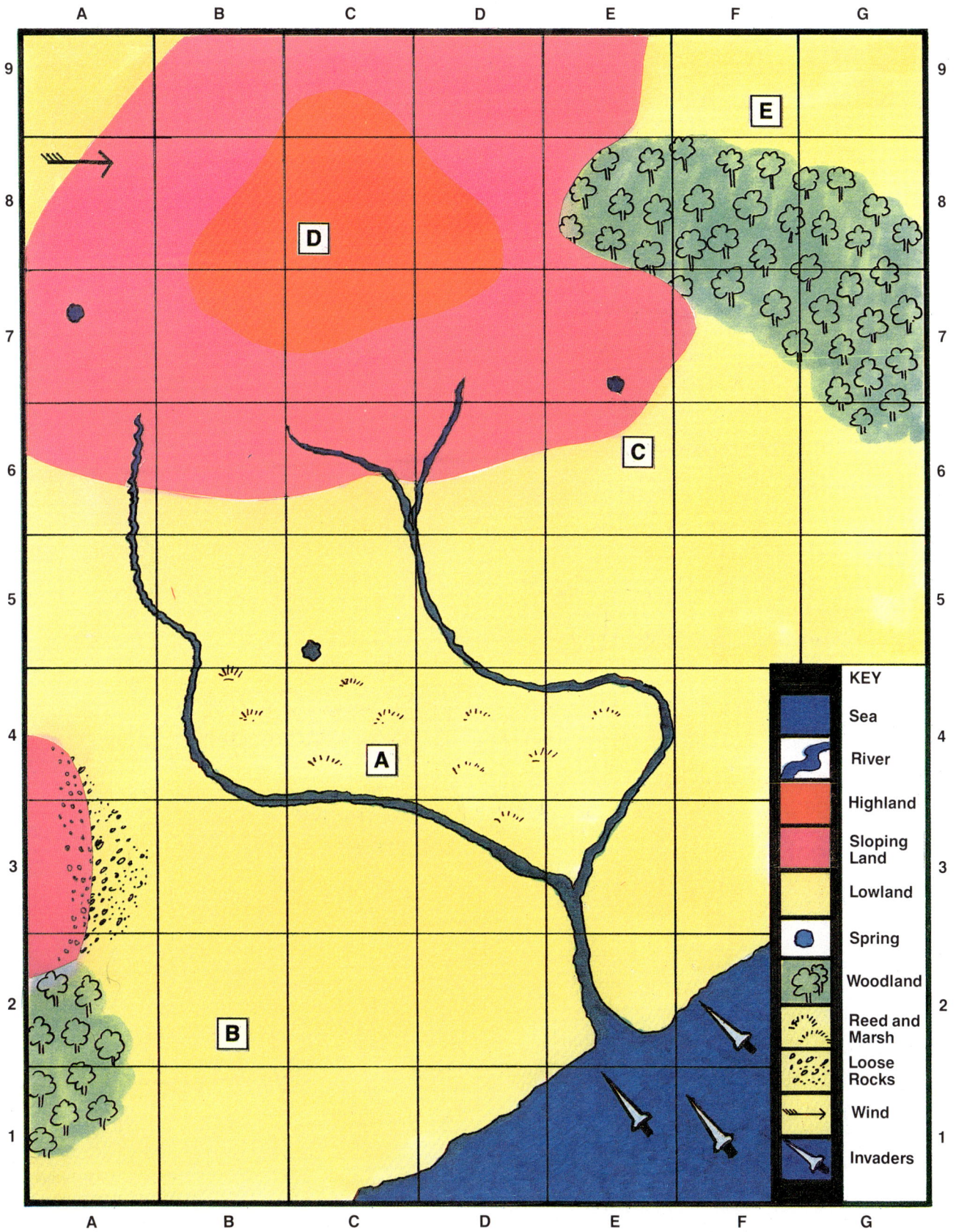

	KEY
	Sea
	River
	Highland
	Sloping Land
	Lowland
	Spring
	Woodland
	Reed and Marsh
	Loose Rocks
	Wind
	Invaders

Settlements developed for many reasons other than farming. Settlements grew up where roads crossed as more and more people moved from one area to another for trade. Other settlements were established at fords (where a river is shallow enough to cross) and at bridges. Such settlements were excellent places for buying and selling, markets could be held there and inns were built for travellers. Mining settlements developed where metals, coal or stone could be dug from the ground. Fishing settlements grew at safe harbours.

Look at this list of settlement locations:

- Where a river or stream is shallow enough to be crossed (ford)
- On a hill which can be defended
- Where two routes (tracks/roads) meet
- Near to minerals which can be dug from the ground
- Where a river meets the sea
- Where a river is narrow and can be crossed by a bridge

Assignment A

Look carefully at the settlements shown on the *oblique* view.

1. Write a sentence about each settlement saying why you think it was located in its particular place e.g. Settlement **A** developed here because it is on a ford.

2. Select the village where you would be most likely to find the following occupations:

   a) Sailmaker   — Village **C** , **B** or **F** ?

   b) Auctioneer   — Village **B** , **E** or **F** ?

   c) Miner   — Village **A** , **D** or **B** ?

   d) Boatbuilder   — Village **E** , **C** or **D** ?

One step further A

1. Which settlements would be most affected by the following? Give your reasons.

   a) Torrential rain caused the rivers to burst their banks.

   b) There was no coal left to be mined.

   c) There was no longer any threat of invasion.

   d) Storms destroyed the fishing boats.

2. Imagine you were a member of a family affected by one of these events. Describe what happened, how you felt, and the results on your life.

3. Sometimes place names describe locations. Can you match the villages on the oblique view with these names: Coalville, Longford, Bridgetown, Sunnyhill, Eastport and Four Lane Ends.

PLACE NAMES AS EVIDENCE

Place names provide us with *evidence* about the history of settlements and the people who named them. Many settlements in Britain were named by immigrants from Europe: Romans, Angles, Saxons, Vikings, Normans and others. The oldest place names are Celtic, most of these are in West Britain where the invaders did not settle in large numbers.

PEOPLE	WORD	MEANING	EXAMPLE
Celtic	pen kil dun llan caer	hill church fort parish fort	Penrith Kilmarnock Dundee Llandudno Caernarfon
Roman	chester caster cester	camp camp camp	Winchester Doncaster Towcester
Saxon	ton ham ing ley field	village village people clearing in forest clearing	Bolton Fulham Reading Leyland Sheffield
Viking	by thorpe	village village	Rugby Scunthorpe

Assignment B

Look at the place name chart. Classify these places by putting them into the correct column in the table.

CELTIC	ROMAN	SAXON	VIKING
Llangollen			

Llangollen
Kildare
Macclesfield
Penrith
Enfield
Taunton
Manchester
Cheltenham
Dundalk
Grimsby
Colchester
Llanberis
Lancaster
Dunfermline
Camberley
Brighton
Cirencester
Nottingham
Cleethorpes
Penmaenmawr
Killarney
Caerphilly
Gillingham
Dunoon
Oldham
Tadcaster
Gloucester
Burnley
Derby

One step further B

These three cartoons represent Oldham, Oxford and Belfast. Can you match the name to the cartoon?

A

C

B

Now draw your own cartoon to illustrate place names. Try them out on a friend.

Personal Research

1 Research the origins of the names of:

  a) The settlement in which your school is located.

  b) The settlement in which you live.

  c) The nearest large city.

  d) Two local villages.

2 Think carefully about your own settlement. Has it always been spelt the same way? Does the name tell you about its past?

3 Use a map of the British Isles. Look for patterns of settlement. Do the place names in certain areas provide evidence of large scale immigrant settlement?

Each picture has a red line on it—this line marks a boundary each time.

This is a plan of Justine's bedroom.

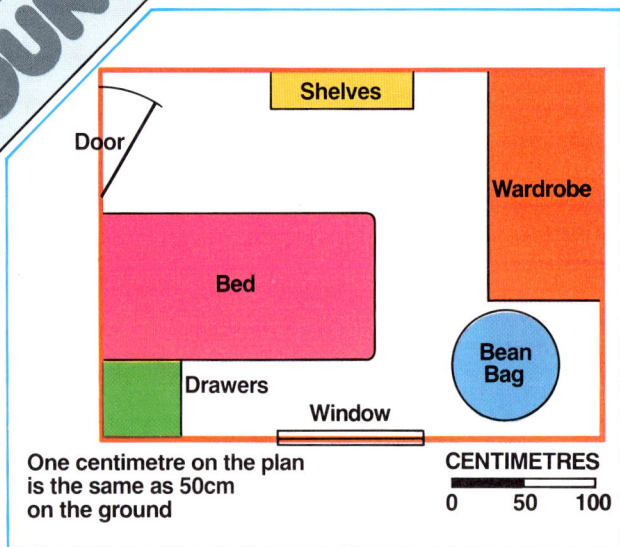

Shelves

Door

Wardrobe

Bed

Bean Bag

Drawers

Window

One centimetre on the plan is the same as 50cm on the ground

CENTIMETRES
0   50   100

This is a plan view of her house and garden.

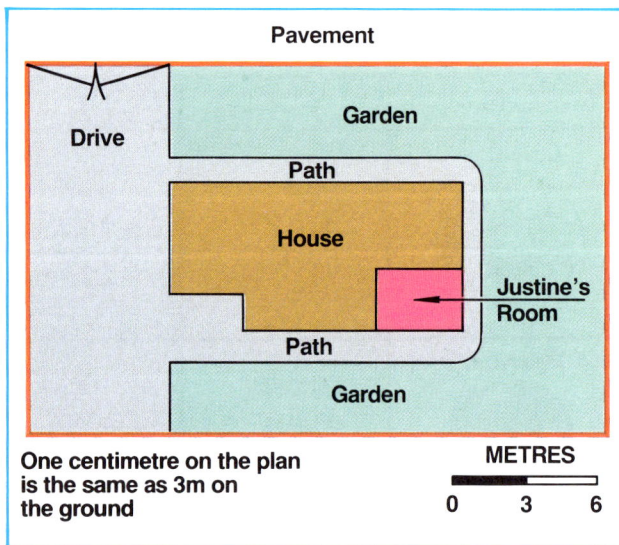

Pavement

Drive

Garden

Path

House

Justine's Room

Path

Garden

One centimetre on the plan is the same as 3m on the ground

METRES
0   3   6

Assignment

1 a) Draw Justine's bedroom plan on the scale 1cm=1 metre.
   b) Draw a plan of your desk top on the scale 1cm=10 cm.

2 a) Measure the school playground. What scale is needed to draw the plan on squared paper 30cm×20cm?
   b) Now choose the best scale for paper 15cm×10cm.

3 a) In which local government area is your school?
   b) In which county do you live?
   c) Use an atlas to name three other counties near to your own.

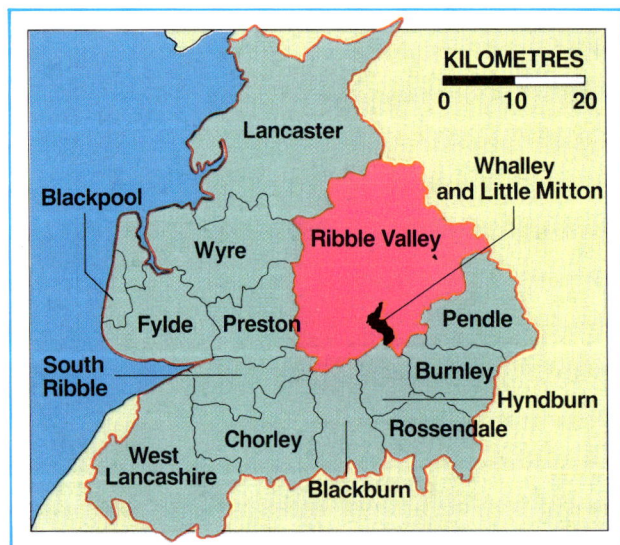

KILOMETRES
0   10   20

Lancaster

Blackpool

Whalley and Little Mitton

Wyre

Ribble Valley

Fylde   Preston

Pendle

South Ribble

Burnley

Hyndburn

Chorley

Rossendale

West Lancashire

Blackburn

The Ribble Valley is one of 14 Local Government Areas in the **county** of Lancashire.

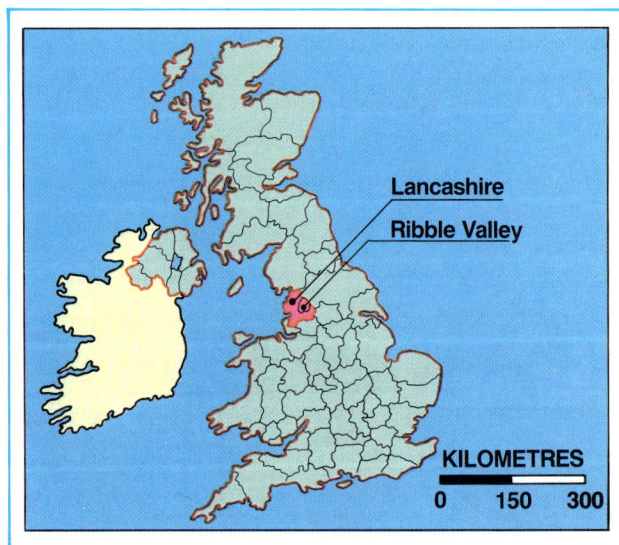

Lancashire

Ribble Valley

KILOMETRES
0   150   300

Lancashire is one of the counties of England.

England, Northern Ireland, Scotland and Wales are all **countries.** Together they make the United Kingdom.

The red line marks the boundary of the family's land. The area in which Justine lives is called Whalley.

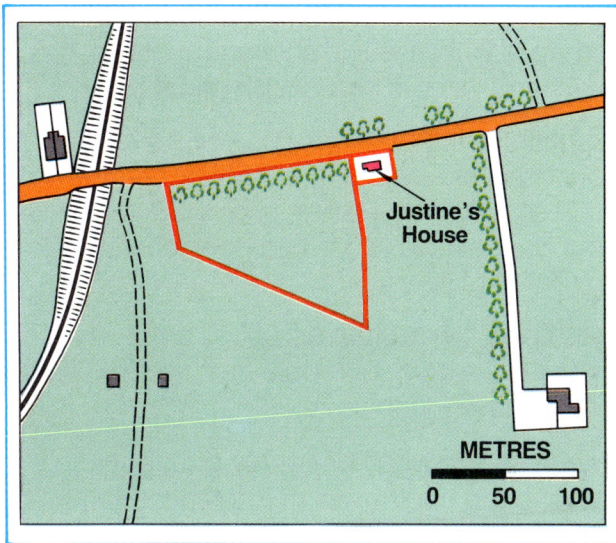

Whalley is a small settlement in the local government area of Ribble Valley.

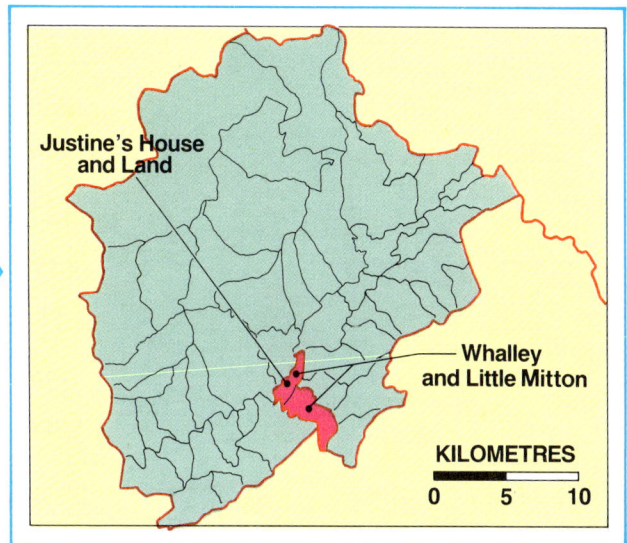

One step further

You will need an atlas.

1 a) Which county is west of Clwyd?

b) Name six counties which share boundaries with Oxfordshire.

2 a) Which is the most westerly English county?

b) In which part of the U.K. is County Antrim?

3 a) In which Scottish region is Edinburgh?

b) Using the first letters complete the name of the countries of Europe.

c) Now name the continents.

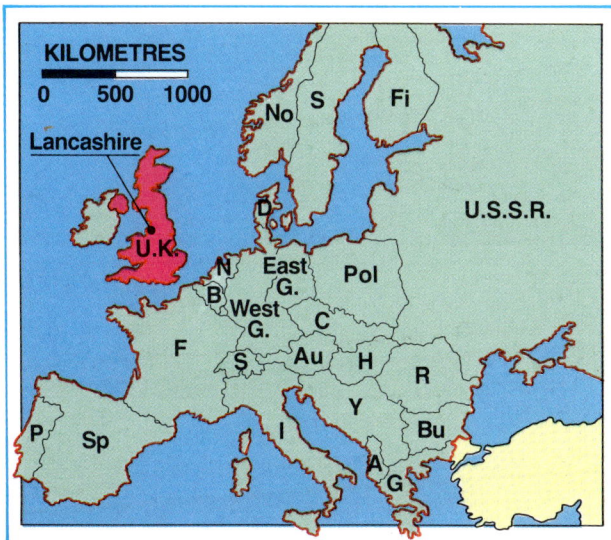

The U.K. is one of the many countries in the **continent** of Europe.

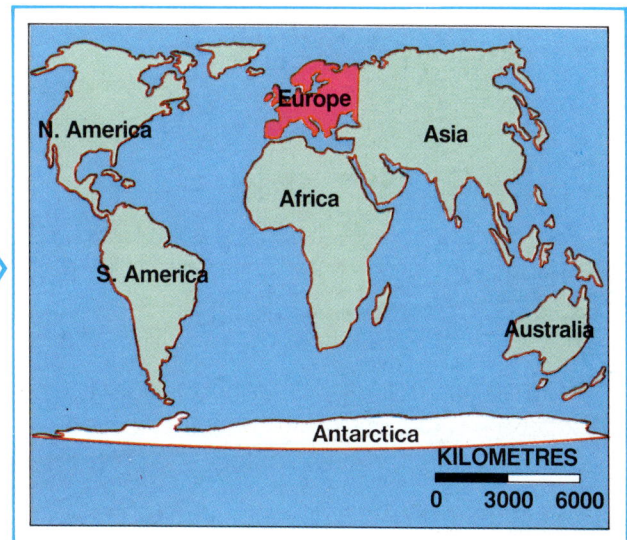

Europe is one of the world's seven continents.

BOUNDARIES IN BRITAIN

A map of Britain which shows the counties is called a **political** map. The lines drawn on it separate one county from another. If we visit the actual boundary between two counties we will not find a line painted on the ground itself.

A map of Britain which shows mountains, hills, rivers and lakes is called a **physical** map.

Sometimes the boundary between two counties is drawn along a physical feature, such as a river or a range of hills. Such physical boundaries have separated people for hundreds of years.

In the past it was often difficult to cross rivers or mountain ranges so people on opposite sides did not have much contact.

When we compare a political map with a physical map we can see whether county boundaries follow physical boundaries. Look at these two maps showing the south-west of England.

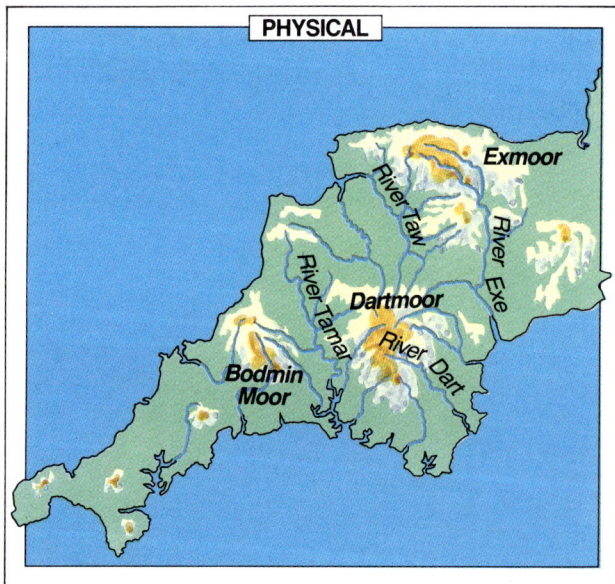

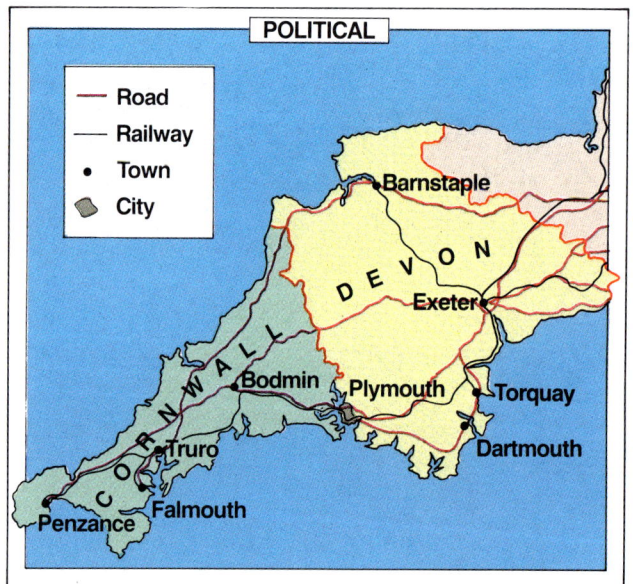

Assignment A

1 Why do you think the county boundary separating Devon and Cornwall has been drawn at this particular place?

2 Put yourself in the following situations. Which map will help you, the physical or the political?

   a) It is a lovely afternoon and a friend suggests a walk in the hills.

   b) A lorry driver stops and asks you directions to Plymouth.

   c) You need to catch the train to London urgently.

   d) You have taken your fishing rod on holiday—where can you find good fishing?

   e) Which is the quickest road to the coast?

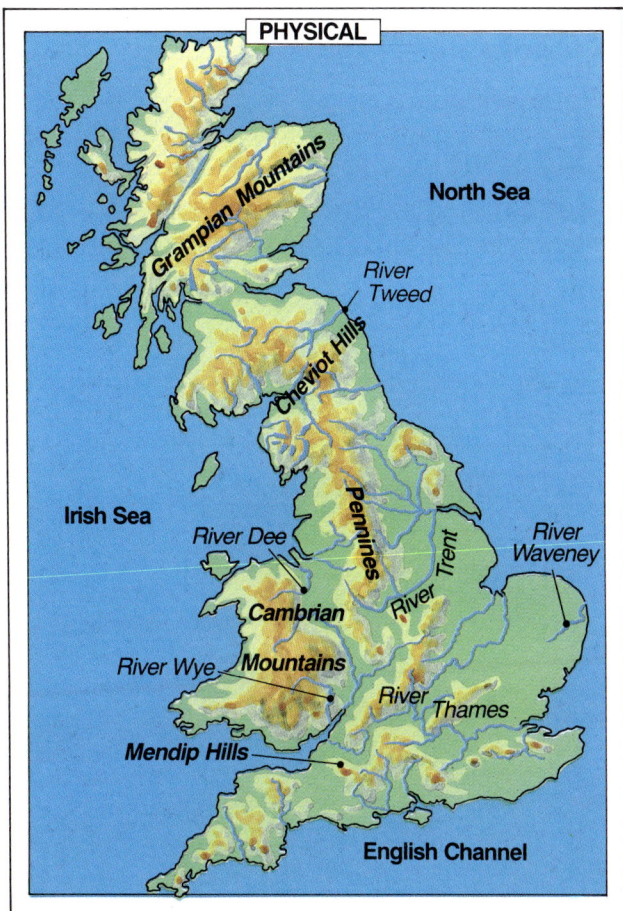

PHYSICAL

Grampian Mountains

North Sea

River Tweed

Cheviot Hills

Irish Sea

Pennines

River Dee

River Trent

River Waveney

Cambrian

River Wye

Mountains

River Thames

Mendip Hills

English Channel

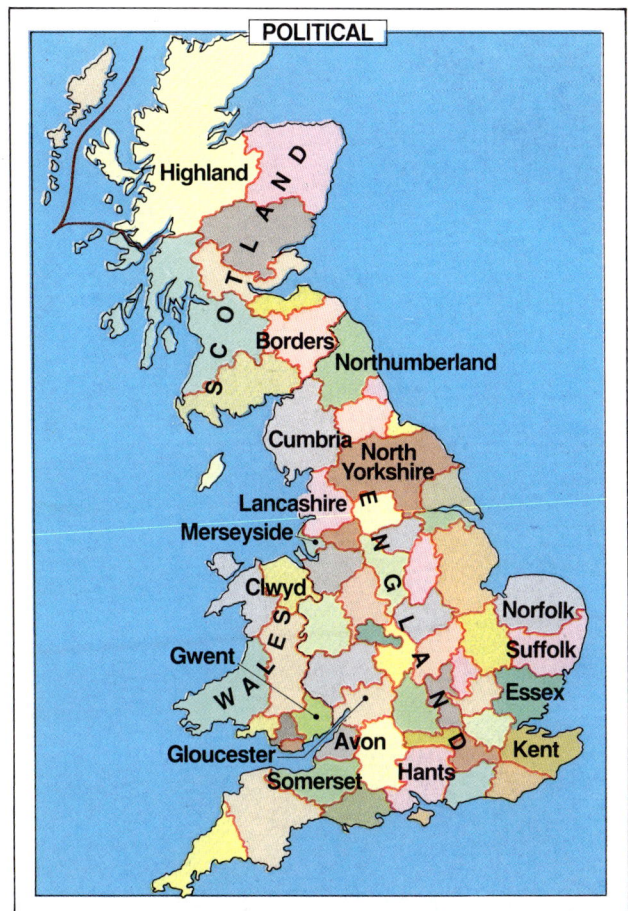

POLITICAL

Highland

SCOTLAND

Borders

Northumberland

Cumbria

North Yorkshire

Lancashire

Merseyside

ENGLAND

Clwyd

Norfolk

WALES

Suffolk

Gwent

Essex

Gloucester

Avon

Kent

Somerset

Hants

Assignment B

1 Use the political and physical maps of Britain to find the rivers which form part of the boundaries between the following counties:

 a) Essex and Kent

 b) Northumberland and the Borders

 c) Merseyside and Clwyd

 d) Gwent and Gloucester

 e) Norfolk and Suffolk

2 Name the hills which separate the following counties:

 a) Lancashire and North Yorkshire

 b) Northumberland and the Borders

 c) Somerset and Avon

Personal Research

1 Look carefully at a map of your local area. Are any of the local government boundaries drawn along physical boundaries?

2 Which counties border on your county? Do any hills or rivers mark the borders?

3 Which county would you choose to visit if your hobby was:

 a) Mountaineering

 b) Water ski-ing on lakes

 c) Collecting seashells

4 The boundaries of the counties of Britain were changed in 1974. Try to obtain an atlas published before 1974 and compare the old counties with the new ones.

 Have any names disappeared?

 Are there any new counties?

BOUNDARIES AROUND THE WORLD

¡Buenos dias!

Bonjour!

Countries are sometimes separated by physical boundaries.

A great river or massive mountain range can separate people completely. Over hundreds of years people living on opposite sides of mountain ranges develop different languages, different foods, clothes and customs.

Look at this picture of two people separated by the Pyrénées Mountains.

Can you work out what each person is saying?

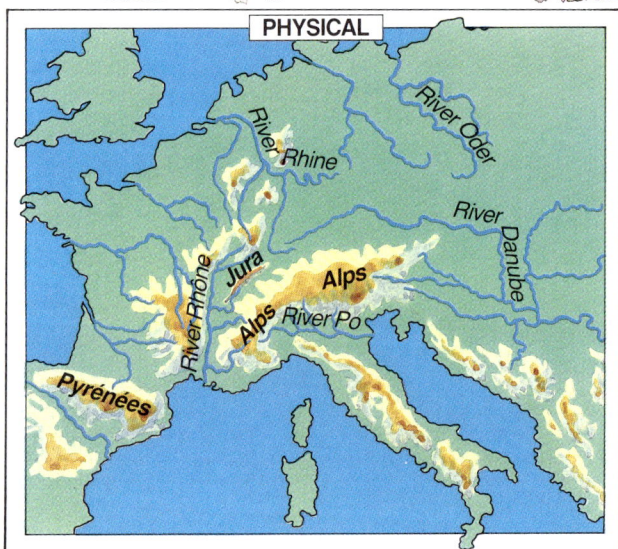

PHYSICAL

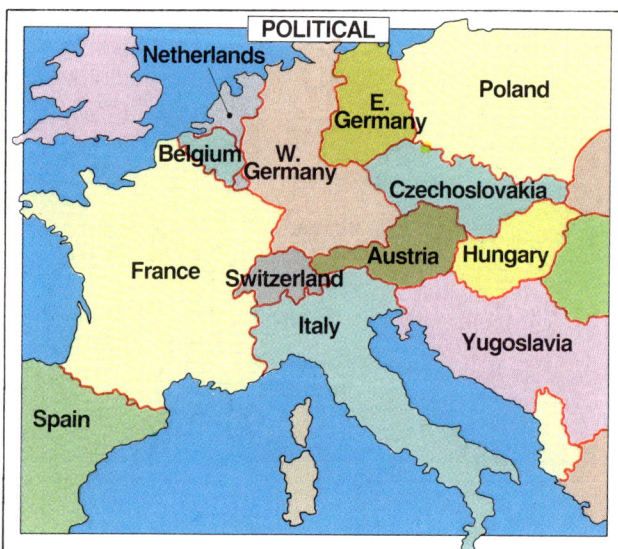

POLITICAL

Assignment A

Now compare the physical map of part of Western Europe with the map showing countries (the political map).

1 Which mountain ranges separate

   a) Spain and France?

   b France and Italy?

   c) Italy and Switzerland?

   d) France and Switzerland?

2 Which rivers form part of the boundary between

   a) France and West Germany?

   b) Switzerland and West Germany?

   c) Poland and East Germany?

Personal Research A

Use physical and political maps of North and South America to find:

1 The rivers which form part of the boundaries between:

   a) Mexico and U.S.A.

   b) Argentina and Uruguay

   c) Brazil and Bolivia

   d) Paraguay and Argentina

2 What physical feature separates Chile and Argentina?

3 Find the 'Great Lakes' in North America. How many lakes are there? Which two countries do they separate?

Look at this map of Australia which shows the physical and political boundaries. The lines which separate the states are mostly straight lines. They do not follow physical features.

Australia was settled by Europeans in the last century. The people who decided on the state boundaries simply drew lines on a map—to them Australia was one country, a new land that could be divided in a simple way.

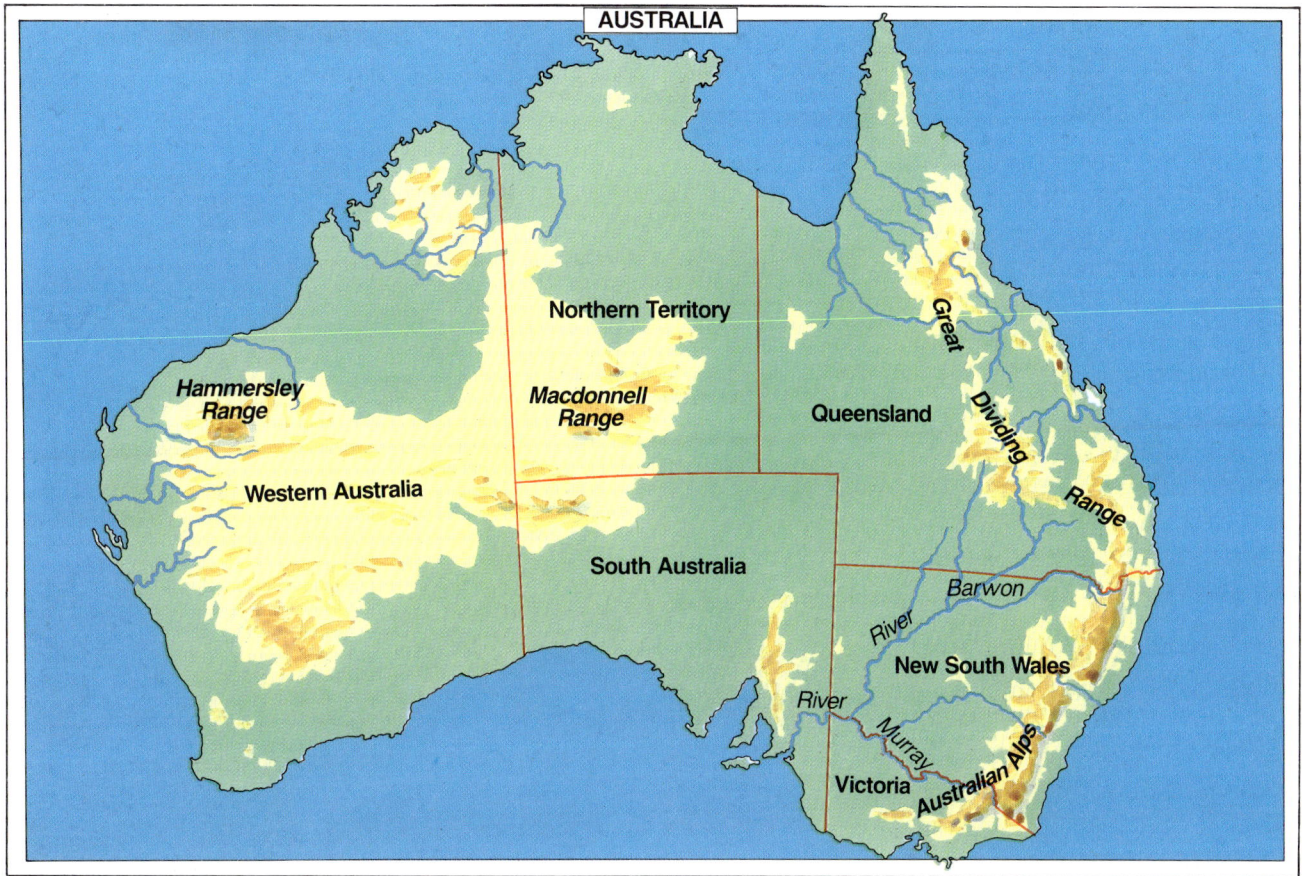

AUSTRALIA

Northern Territory

Hammersley Range

Macdonnell Range

Great Dividing Range

Queensland

Western Australia

South Australia

Barwon

River

New South Wales

River

Murray

Australian Alps

Victoria

Assignment B

Not all Australia's state boundaries are straight. Some in the first part of the country to be settled by Europeans follow physical features.

1 Which states have boundaries following physical features?

2 Which river separates Victoria from New South Wales?

3 Which river forms part of the boundary between Queensland and New South Wales?

4 Does the boundary between Northern Territory and Western Australia follow physical features?

Personal Research B

When newcomers settled or conquered a country they often drew straight lines for boundaries. Sometimes this ignores rivers, mountains and the people who live there.

1 Use a map of the U.S.A. Look at the pattern of the state boundaries.

a) Is the pattern in the east the same as in the west?

b) Think about the boundaries in Australia, remember the last parts to be settled by Europeans had straight line boundaries. Which part of the U.S.A. do you think was settled last, east or west?

Oh no! If only these town folk would take their litter back home! They don't think about the danger to animals.

I've had such a lovely day Daddy.

Why can't we stay for the weekend? I want to, can we?

The Watson family love to drive past green fields and wide open spaces. They have decided that they would like a house in the country where they could stay at weekends and during their summer holidays.

The Watsons have bought a cottage in a lovely old village. A local family, the Plows, was hoping to buy the cottage. The Watsons could afford to pay more. The Plows cannot afford a house in the village. Prices have gone up a lot since city families started buying second homes. The Plows realise they will have to leave the village where they have always lived and worked.

The Plows children attend the village school. Mrs Plows does most of her shopping at the Post Office Store. The other villagers will miss the Plows - but at least the Watsons are coming.

I wonder if the Watsons will do their shopping here on Saturdays?

I hope the Watsons will send their children to this school! We have fewer each year.

I'm sure they'll buy petrol from me and have their cars serviced here!

Hardly anyone catches my bus any longer!

Assignment A

1 If you were the Watsons would you do your shopping at a supermarket or in the village?

Say why.

2 Will the Watson children attend the village school?

Explain your answer.

3 Imagine you are Mr and Mrs Plows.

Write about how you feel about the Watsons.

4 What will happen to the shop, school, garage and bus service if more families leave the village?

5 Who would be worst affected if the shop and school close, the weekend families or the permanent families?

Assignment B

1 What damage are the Watsons causing to the farmland?

2 List the dangers to land and animals they have caused.

3 How would you feel about the Watsons if you were a farmer.

4 Now read Mrs Watson's complaint to Mrs Payne.

5 What would you say to Mrs Watson if she complained about the noisy tractor?

6 Do you feel sorry that the Watsons can't buy stamps, food or petrol on Saturday? Explain your answer.

7 What happens to pregnant sheep chased by dogs?

David's parents have friends who are farmers. Their son Warren is the same age as David. David and Warren are going to spend a week in each other's homes. Both boys expect the area that they visit will be better than their own.

These pictures and comments show you what they think of town life.

I'm fed up of being made to move to play somewhere else!

How GREAT all those people to play with.

All this traffic! What a noise!

You can travel everywhere by bus. It's so EASY.

Oh .. if the lift is BROKEN we'll have to walk to the top!

I can't wait to get to the top. The view must be SMASHING!

It's GREAT -- so many sports to choose from.

MEGADOME SPORTS HALL

I have to queue for my sport. It takes all my pocket money.

All these factories MUST mean plenty of jobs.

The heavy lorries should NOT be allowed in town. They break the pavements.

My Mum won't let me go to the match because of the fighting.

I wish I lived nearer the ground. I never see the great players.

There are so many shops to choose from.

It's so crowded you can hardly move.

Assignment A

Look carefully at the pictures and the boys' comments. Now complete the chart. Decide who you think said each sentence. Write the comment under the boy's name. Then add your own point of view.

SCENE:	DAVID'S VIEW	WARREN'S VIEW	MY VIEW
1 Street Play	I'm fed up of being told to move away and play somewhere	How great! All those other kids to play football with	I think ... .

Now David and Warren comment on life in the countryside.

I get so bored, sat in a treehouse on my own.

WOW, a tree-house! TARZAN-ROBIN HOOD I cannot wait.

It must be great, living on a farm... All those animals and barns for playing in.

There are so many jobs I have to do every day... MUCKING OUT is WORST!

There is hardly any traffic to worry about.

We are so isolated there are no buses. I hardly ever see my friends.

I have 3 kilometres to walk to school... Some days I get SOAKED.

I bet the walks are PERFECT and the views are SMASHING.

I can't wait to smell the new-mown hay.

The stink from the manure spreader makes me sick.

I love lambs. I'd like one for a pet.

I love lamb, especially with MINT SAUCE!

All those lovely little rabbits and foxes to see.

We have such trouble from pests destroying our crops and killing hens.

Assignment B

Complete a chart for the country area in the same way that you did for the town.

One step further

Look at this list of places and events. Make a new chart.

1 A museum
2 An owl hooting late at night
3 Playground in town
4 Feeding the chickens
5 Cinema/video shop
6 Ice Cream Van
7 Snow

Write what you think David would say and then what Warren would say. Give your own opinion about each of them.

Remember David and Warren may agree on some topics.

THE POSTAL SERVICE

Mr Caine has shown the class how to find **evidence** from a letter.

FIRST LOOK AT THE STAMP. CHECK WHICH COUNTRY IT IS FROM. THEN LOOK AT THE POSTMARK. IT TELLS YOU FOUR THINGS.

Where the letter was posted

The time it was franked

The date of posting

The year of posting

Assignment A

1 Draw the four stamps and label each one with the name of the country.

2 Write four sentences about the postmark.
Begin: **1** This letter was posted in ....

Now look at the postcard David brought to school.

Assignment B

1 What time was the card posted?

2 What day, month and year?

3 What did it cost to post a card then?

4 What does it cost today?

Assignment C

1 In which town was it posted?

2 In which town was it delivered?

3 On which day was it delivered? **clue** ... read the message

4 Would a postcard be delivered as quickly today?

One step further A

1 Ask old people whether the postal service is better or worse than when they were young.

2 What has replaced the letter for sending messages?

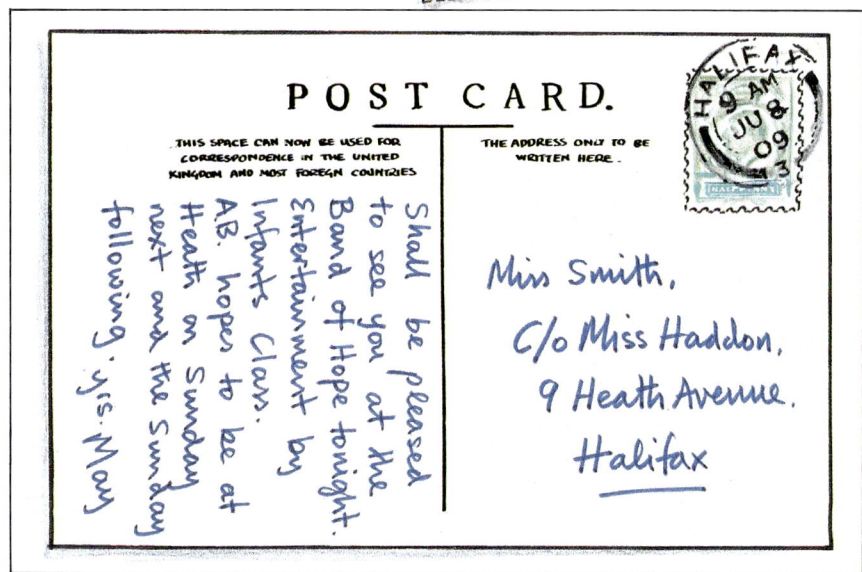

Personal Research

1 Make a class collection of old postcards.

Check the dates and places on the postmark.

What kind of messages did people send?

2 Find out how many collections and deliveries there were each day in your town in the past.

3 Can you discover how long a letter would have taken to reach London from your town in 1909?

Farah's class made a daily collection of envelopes delivered to their homes and school. They made sure the envelopes were empty before they brought them to their teacher. They recorded their findings on this data sheet.

DATA SHEET

Letter	1st class	2nd class	Post Code	Place of posting	Date of posting	Date of delivery	Days taken
1	✓		✓	Oxford	2nd May	3rd May	1
2		✓	✗	Hull	1st May	4th May	3
3			✓	U.S.A.	25th April	4th May	9
4							

One step further B

Make a class collection like Farah's.

1 What is the average time taken for:

   a) First class letters
   b) Second class letters.

2 Do letters with postcodes arrive quicker than letters without? (Remember to compare letters of the same class.)

3 Identify on a map where the letters were posted.

4 Is there a connection between the distance a letter travels and the time it takes?

5 Classify your mail into three sections
   a) local   b) rest of the U.K.   c) abroad
   Is most of your mail a), b) or c)?

Postmen and postwomen deliver letters to people all over Britain.

Penny Black delivers letters to farms and villages.

Here is a letter Penny has been asked to deliver.

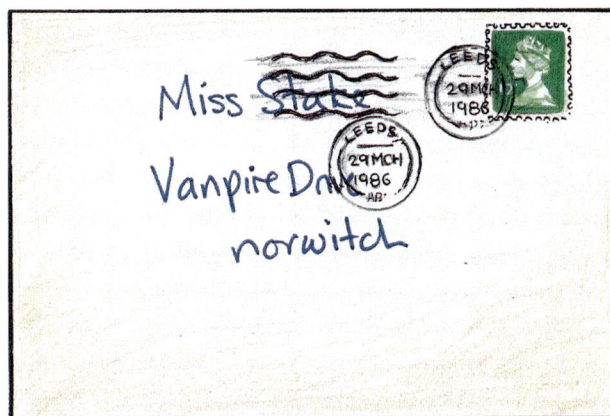

Assignment D

1 Why is Penny unhappy with this letter?

2 Address a letter to yourself that Penny would be happy with.

Saul Stamp gets up at 5 a.m. He arrives at the sorting office by 6 a.m. in order to start work. He sorts out his letters and puts them in order, house by house and street by street. The map shows his delivery round.

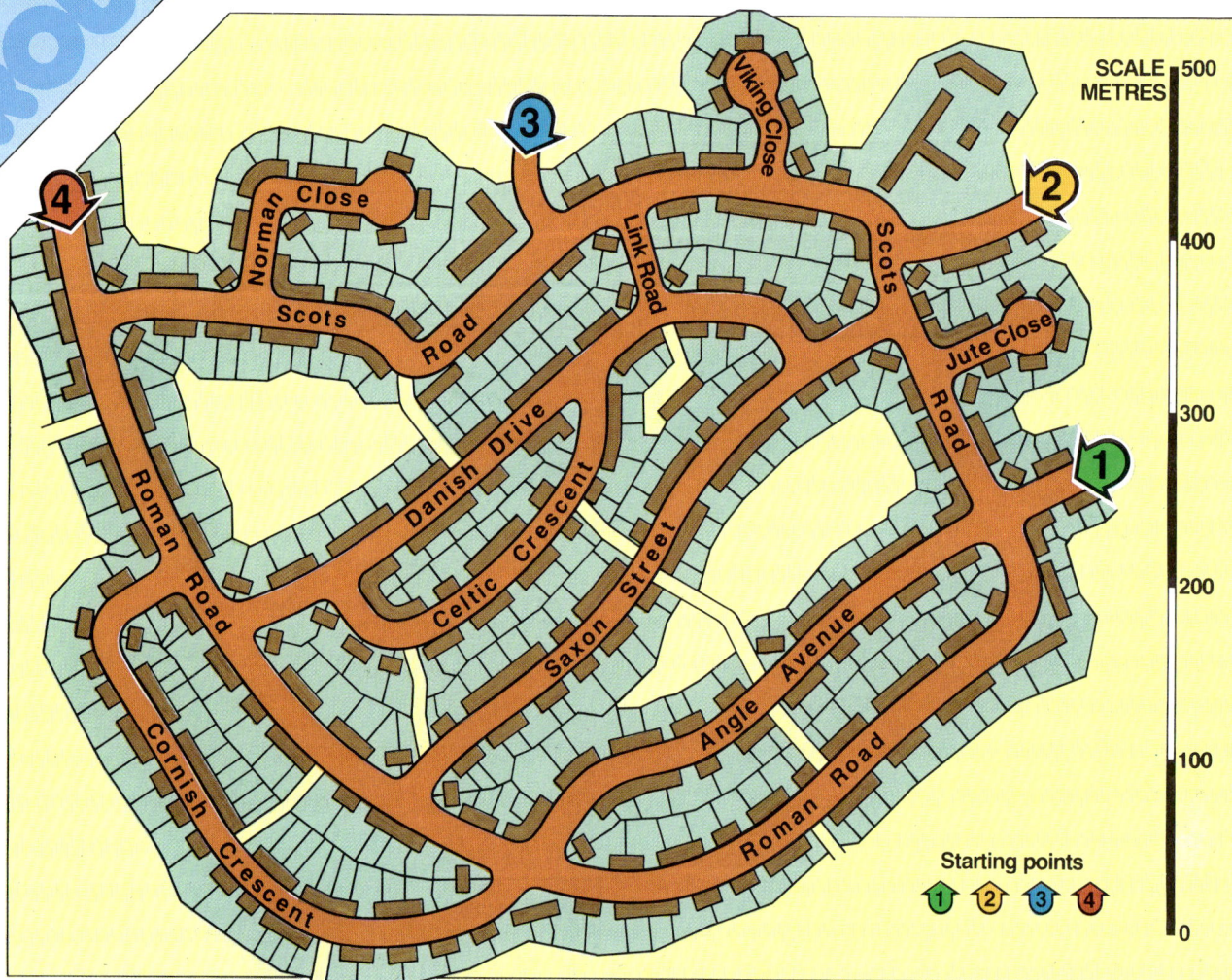

Assignment A

1 Work out a good route for Mr Stamp. Choose any one of the starting points and make sure you go along every road at least once.

2 When you have drawn your route, work out how long the route is in kilometres and metres. One way of doing this is by laying a piece of wool or string along your route and using the scale line.

3 When other children in your class have made their routes, compare the lengths of string. Who found the shortest route?

4 What is a cul-de-sac?

Can you name one on the map?

5 What are the circular areas for at the ends of cul-de-sacs?

6 Draw the shape of a crescent.

7 Mr Stamp walks this post round every day from Monday to Saturday whatever the weather, and then he does other jobs when he gets back to the post office. Can you think of a time of the year when he will need extra help?

This map shows part of Penny's round. She delivers the mail to all the farms and villages in a country area.

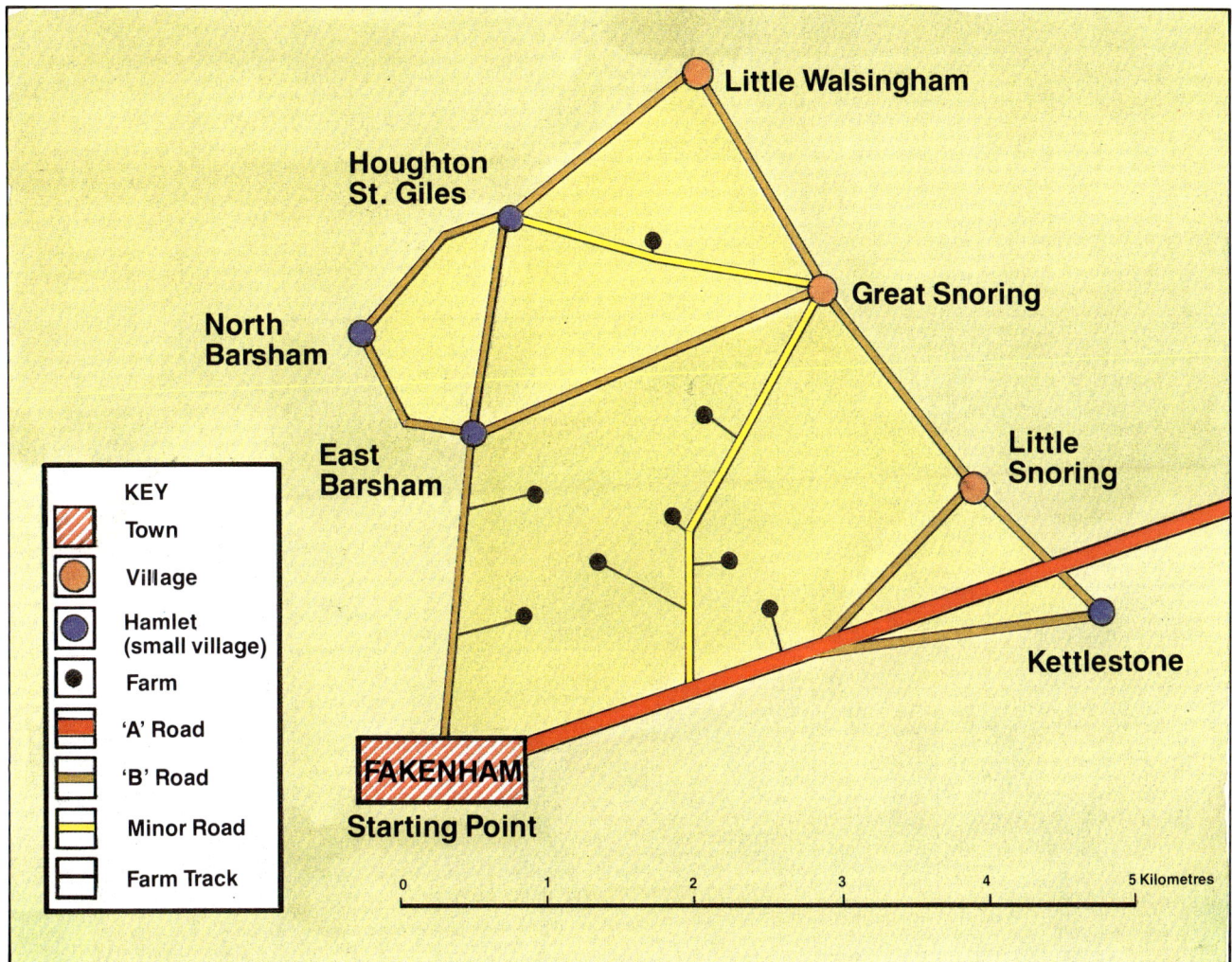

KEY

- Town
- Village
- Hamlet (small village)
- Farm
- 'A' Road
- 'B' Road
- Minor Road
- Farm Track

Little Walsingham

Houghton St. Giles

North Barsham

Great Snoring

Little Snoring

East Barsham

Kettlestone

FAKENHAM
Starting Point

0   1   2   3   4   5 Kilometres

Assignment B

1   Work out a good route for Penny. She begins each day in Fakenham.

2   How many kilometres will she drive using your route?

3   Compare the distance she travels on your route with the distance she travels on a friend's route.

One step further

1   Who travels the furthest Penny or Saul?

2   Who walks the furthest?

3   Which post round would you rather work on? Give your reasons.

4   Find out whether people who live in the country receive as many deliveries a day as people who live in towns.

WIND

'Rock a bye baby in the tree top
When the wind blows the cradle will rock'

'When the bough breaks the baby will fall
If only someone had checked the weather
forecast'

The wind can be a nuisance but it can also be a help.
Look at these six pictures.

Assignment A

1   Describe in your own words what each
    picture shows and what effect the wind is
    having.

2   Choose three pictures.

    Draw the scenes that you think will happen
    next.

3   List the six pictures under two headings.
    a) Uses of the wind.
    b) Problems with the wind.

One step further

1   Can you give other examples of the good
    and bad effects of the wind?

2   Draw a picture of each.

    Write a description of how the wind affects
    each event.

3   Find out what the **doldrums** were and why
    sailors hated them.

The strength of the wind can be measured with an **Anemometer**. This helps us to know whether the wind is safe or dangerous.

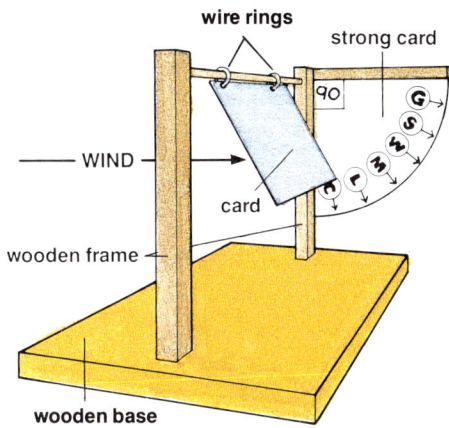

As the wind blows it pushes the piece of card upwards. When there is no wind the card does not move. As the wind gets stronger the card rises higher.

WIND FORCE SCALE

SYMBOL	WIND	WHAT TO LOOK FOR
C →	**C**alm	Smoke goes straight up
L →	**L**ight breeze	You feel the wind on your face
M →	**M**oderate breeze	Paper blows about and small branches sway
W →	**W**indy	Large branches sway
S →	**S**trong wind	Twigs break off branches it is hard to walk against the wind
G →	**G**ale	Damage to buildings and trees are uprooted

1

2

3

4

5

6

Assignment B

Look at the six pictures showing different wind strengths.

1   Draw each picture and label them with the correct symbol.

2   Draw your own picture for the symbols
   C → G → W →

3   What wind strength caused the following:

   a) Miss Happ's washing blew off the line and landed in the fish pond.

   b) David's drawing of his teacher blew out of his hand and in through Mr Caine's window.

As well as knowing how hard the wind blows we should also know the direction it blows from. Sally's class went into the school grounds to look at evidence of wind direction. They stood around an oak tree. It was autumn and the leaves were ready to fall.

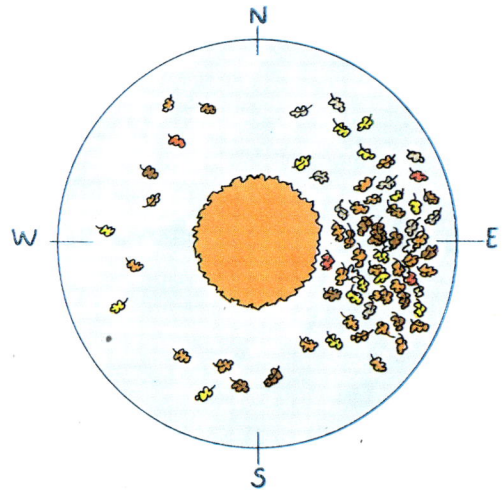

Falling leaves are carried to the ground on the wind.

Each marks where a leaf fell around the oak tree.

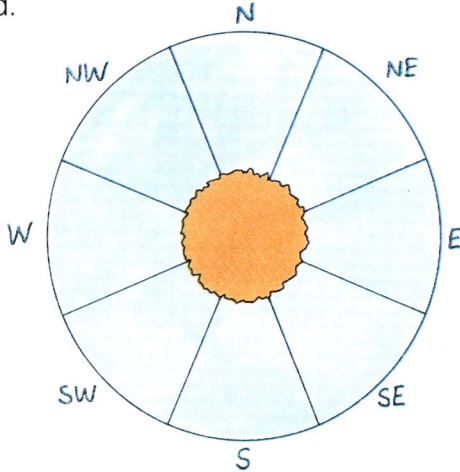

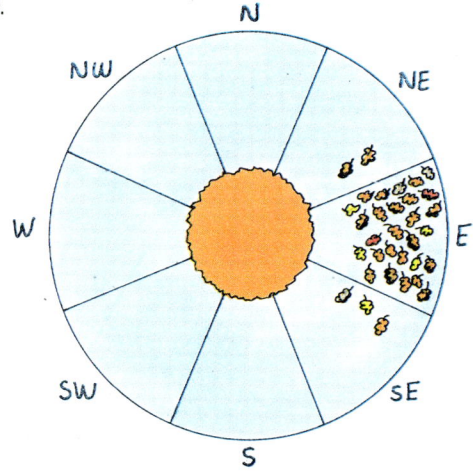

The leaves were cleared. A compass was used to divide up the area.

On Monday most leaves had fallen in the east. The wind must have blown from the west.

Each day the leaves were counted and cleared. The class made this record.
Remember it shows the direction the wind blows **from**.

Assignment A

Monday's plan is shown above.

1 Draw plans of the oak tree for Tuesday, Wednesday, Thursday and Friday. Show on your plans where you think most leaves fell.

2 Draw five plans of your own showing leaf fall. Give them to a partner who will then draw a 5 day chart.

WIND DIRECTION FOR FIVE DAYS

MON.	TUES.	WED.	THURS.	FRI.
W	SW	E	NW	N

Leaves can only help us in the autumn. We need a weather vane to tell us wind direction throughout the year. The arrow points to where the wind is blowing **from**.

Sally used a home-made weather vane to record the wind direction every day for two weeks. She chalked the compass points on the ground. Each day she recorded the direction the arrow pointed.

Assignment B

Sally recorded the wind for 14 days. Look at the boxes she shaded in the first diagram.

1 On how many days:

a) was there no wind?
b) did the wind blow from the north?

2 From which direction:

b) did the wind never blow?
c) did the wind blow most often?

For 14 days, she shaded in one box for each day the wind blew from a particular direction.

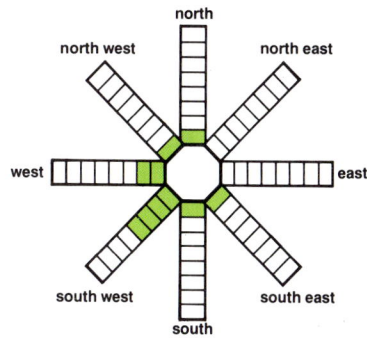

Sally also looked for weather patterns. She kept a 28 day record. When the wind blew but brought no rain she coloured the box red. When the wind blew and brought rain she used blue.

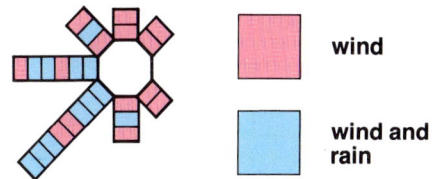

- wind
- wind and rain

Assignment C

Sally recorded weather patterns for 28 days.

1 How many days had ...

a) wind without rain?
b) wind and rain?
c) no wind?

2 From which direction did ...

a) rain not come during the month?
b) the wettest winds come?

3 Should Sally carry an umbrella if ...

a) her wind vane points 'N'?
b) her wind vane points 'S.W.'?

One step further

1 Record the wind and rain for 28 days and make a wind/rain rose of your own.

2 Which is the most common direction for the wind to blow in your area?

3 Compare your pattern with Sally's.

No matter how hard you look you will never see the wind. It is invisible. You can feel it, you may hear it and you will certainly observe its effects, but you will never see it.

The wind is air that is on the move. To some the wind is a friend. It brings rain for the crops, it carries seeds and birds, it dries washing on the line. To others the wind is a foe. It can drive sand into the eyes of travellers, it demolishes houses and makes families homeless, it can even kill people.

THE HURRICANE IS MOVING WEST AT A SPEED OF 400KM AN HOUR. ALREADY 200 HOUSES HAVE BEEN DESTROYED. THE NUMBER OF DEAD AND HOMELESS CONTINUES TO RISE.

OH NO! IT'S HEADING OUR WAY.

Assignment A

1 When a hurricane approaches people should take cover and be prepared to live for up to 3 days until the rescue services can arrive. Look at the objects in the picture.

Which would you take to the shelter with you?

List them in order of importance.

2 Imagine you are in the U.S.A. and hear a hurricane approaching. Your parents are away. Describe your feelings.
What would you do? Would you try to escape? What about sisters, brothers and pets.

This photograph shows a traditional windmill that is still in use.

Windmills have been used for hundreds of years for grinding corn and for pumping water. In Britain they have been replaced with engines that use other sources of energy. One problem with energy produced from gas, oil or coal is that the fuel cannot be replaced. It is also expensive. How is the wind different?

This is an **aerogenerator** a modern type of windmill. The wind turns the blades and they **generate** electricity.

Assignment B

1   Choose a windy day. Walk around your school grounds with your anemometer. Find the windiest spot and the least windy spot.

    Where would you erect an aerogenerator if you had one for your school?

2   Now look at the windrose for your school. Is the place you have chosen facing in the direction from which the wind usually blows?

Personal Research

Today many people enjoy sailing and wind-surfing. In the past great sailing ships depended on wind. These ships were replaced by others which used an alternative form of power.

1   When were the great sailing ships replaced?

2   What power replaced sail?

3   Why was it regarded as better?

4   What sources of power do modern ships use?

HEATHROW

The Johnson family has been invited to spend a holiday with Jo and Ellie in Vermont, U.S.A. They have saved up all year in order to pay for what should be the holiday of a lifetime. Mr and Mrs Johnson know that flights across the Atlantic are cheaper in winter but they decided they wanted to go in summer.

Can you guess why?

Eventually they flew from Heathrow Airport on June 20th. They were told to check-in for their flight at 19.15.

Assignment A

Mr and Mrs Johnson had to decide the best way of travelling to Heathrow. Baby Johnson can travel free.

1 In order to arrive at Heathrow in time for the flight

   a) Which train would they catch?
   b) Which coach would they catch?

2 Which takes longer the coach or the train journey?

3 What will the total cost for the family be

   a) By train?   b) By coach?

4 Copy and complete the chart.

	Cost for family	Time	Advantages	Disadvantages
Bus				
Rail				

One step further A

1 Which do you think would be the more comfortable journey?

2 Why do you think it costs more to travel by train?

3 Which form of transport would you choose? Give your reasons.

4 Why should children and senior citizens travel at reduced prices?

Coach Timetable

Depart	Arrive
PRESTON	HEATHROW AIRPORT
08·00	14·10
10·00	16·10
12·00	18·10
14·00	20·10
Change coach in London	

Rail Timetable

Depart	Arrive
PRESTON	HEATHROW AIRPORT
04·09	08·25
07·09	11·05
07·53	12·05
14·55	19·05
15·36	19·35
Change coach at Watford	

Return Fares in £'s

	By Coach	By Rail
Adults	18·00	22·00
Children	12·00	11·00
Senior citizens	12·00	22·00

Mrs Johnson decided to work out how much it would cost to drive to Heathrow. The family owns an Austin Montego. She knows it will travel 60 km on 5 litres of petrol. The distance from Preston to Heathrow is 360 km. Allowing for stops the family travels 60 km every hour.

Hours	Distance in km	Litres	Cost £
1	60	5	2·25
2			
3			
4			
5			
6			

Assignment B

1 Complete the chart.

2 How long will the journey take?

3 How much will a single journey cost?

4 How much will the return journey cost?

One step further B

1 Complete the chart for journeys from other parts of Britain to Heathrow.

	Distance in km	Litres	Cost in £	Time Taken
Aberdeen	780	65	29·25	13 hours
Glasgow				
Bristol				
Holyhead				
Dover				

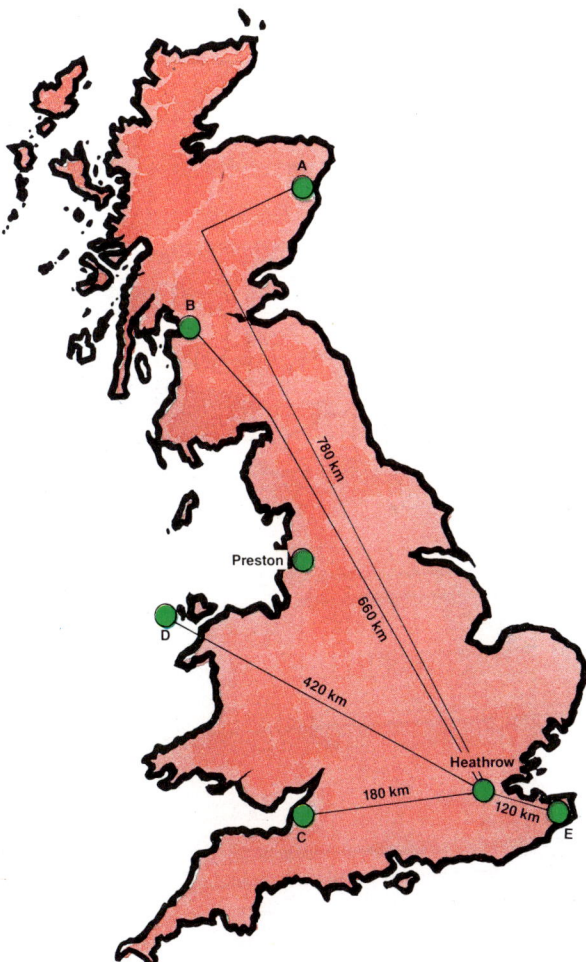

2 Which form of transport would you choose? The more money you save the more you will have to spend in the U.S.A. but you may prefer greater comfort and convenience. Discuss this with a group of friends.

3 Now use the information to work out the cost for one adult by a) car b) train c) coach.
Does this change your opinion of the best form of travel?

Personal Research

1 Use maps and local information to discover the costs of a journey to Heathrow for your family.

2 The Johnsons could have flown to New York from Manchester. Find out which other U.K. airports have direct flights to the U.S.A.

Map labels: A, B, Preston, D, C, Heathrow, E, 780 km, 660 km, 420 km, 180 km, 120 km

CROSSING THE ATLANTIC

The Johnson family is about to cross the Atlantic Ocean on the journey to Vermont. The trip will take about six hours. In the past the journey took much longer and could often be hazardous.

Assignment A

1. How long did each of these aircraft take to cross the Atlantic?
   a) Vimy   b) Jumbo   c) Concorde

2. How many kilometres per hour does each aeroplane average?

3. Complete the sentence : 'Compared with the past, flights across the Atlantic are . . .' *(faster/slower)*

Personal Research A

1. Who flew the Vickers Vimy in 1919?

2. What award did they receive?

3. Where did they take off and land?

1. Which two countries built Concordes?

Assignment B

1. How long was the Mayflower at sea?

2. How was the Mayflower powered?

3. How many km a day did each ship average?

4. Modern ships cross the Atlantic more *(quickly/slowly)* than ships in the past.

Personal Research B

1. How many people travelled in the Mayflower?

2. What was their destination?

3. Where did they eventually land?

4. Which was the largest passenger ship ever to cross the Atlantic?

FLYING ACROSS THE ATLANTIC

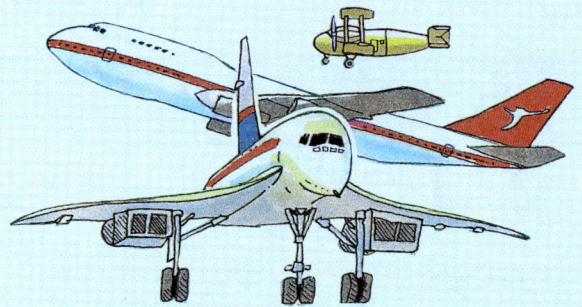

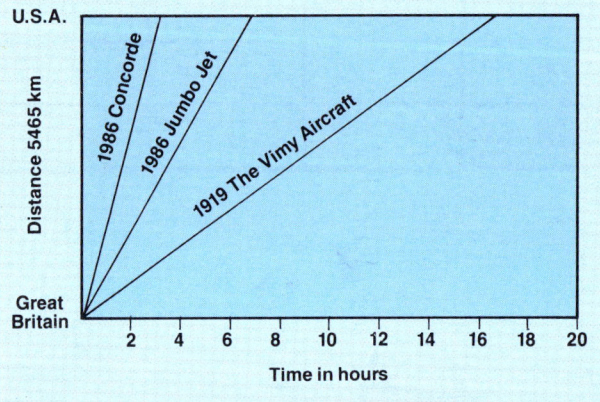

U.S.A.
Distance 5465 km
- 1986 Concorde
- 1986 Jumbo Jet
- 1919 The Vimy Aircraft

Great Britain

Time in hours: 2 4 6 8 10 12 14 16 18 20

SAILING ACROSS THE ATLANTIC

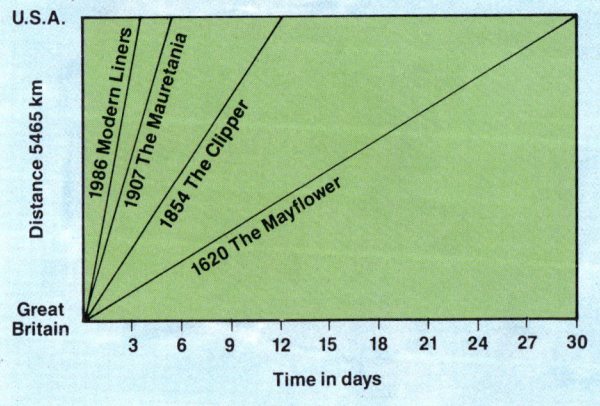

U.S.A.
Distance 5465 km
- 1986 Modern Liners
- 1907 The Mauretania
- 1854 The Clipper
- 1620 The Mayflower

Great Britain

Time in days: 3 6 9 12 15 18 21 24 27 30

Leaving the Country

All governments have rules about who can enter their country. A **passport** is usually necessary for travel between countries. Some governments, including the U.S.A., issue an entry permit **(visa)** to visitors. Look at the pictures which show what the Johnson family did before boarding the plane.

TERMINAL ENTRANCE

TICKET CHECK-IN + SCALES

BAR

SECURITY

PASSPORT CONTROL

DUTY FREE SHOP

BOARDING + FINAL SECURITY

Assignment C

1 Describe the family's journey from arrival to the 'plane.

2 Why are symbols very important at International airports?

3 Draw the symbol the family would look for if they wanted: a meal, first-aid, to post a letter, to change money.

4 What do the other 12 symbols tell you?

Personal Research C

1 What is a duty free shop?

2 Find the names of 8 airlines which fly the Atlantic.

One step further

1 What might happen if there was no passport control?

2 Why are there security checks?

3 Imagine you had been invited into the cockpit by the pilot. Although it was your first flight you had read a great deal about aeroplanes. The headlines the following day read:

"BRITISH CHILD TAKES OVER FROM SICK PILOT—FLIES PLANE SINGLE-HANDED!"

Write your report of how you saved the plane load of passengers.

VACATION U.S.A.

Sally and David are enjoying their vacation with their Mum and Dad. They are travelling to the western United States to visit three National Parks and three National Monuments. A **National Park** is an area of beauty which people have decided to conserve.

Conservation means keeping an area as natural and unspoilt as possible. In America, the government decides if an area is important enough to be made into a National Park. National Monuments are created by the decision of the President.

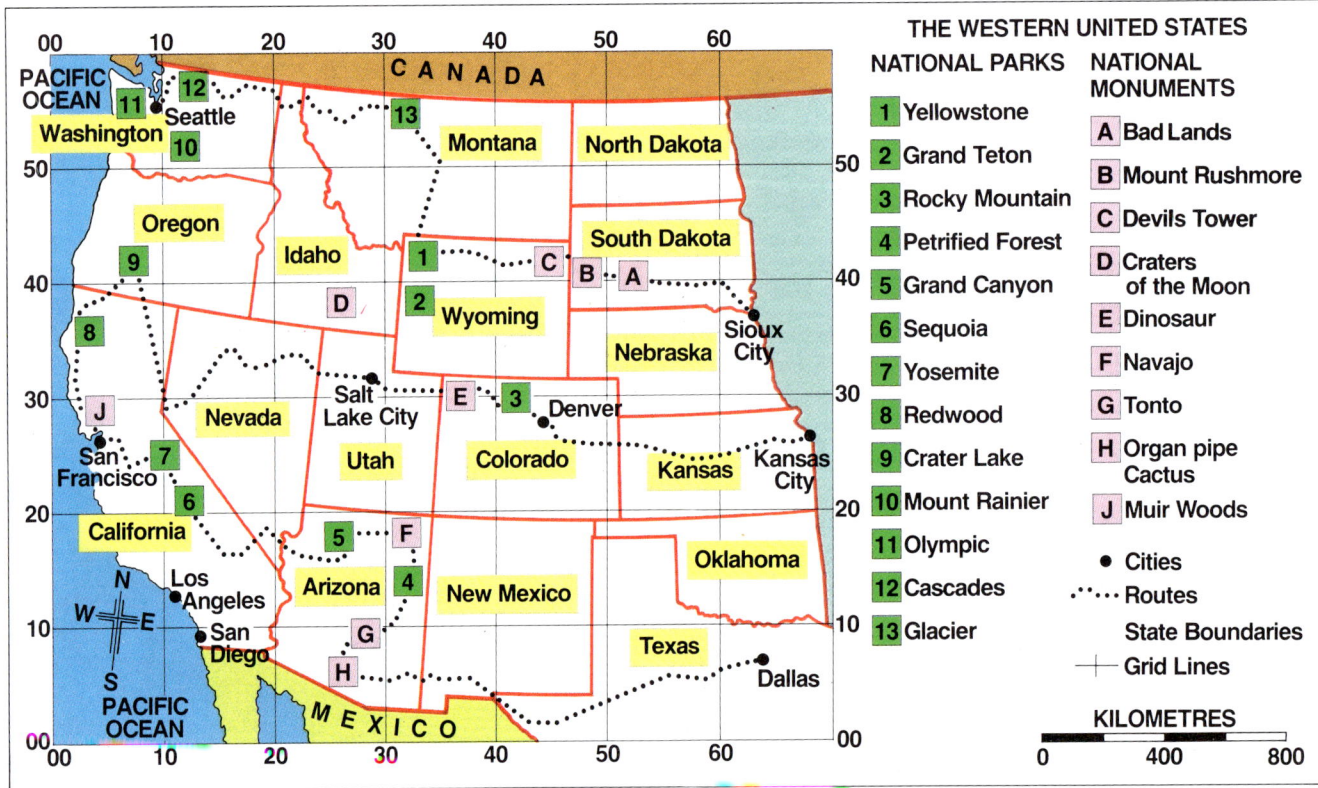

THE WESTERN UNITED STATES

NATIONAL PARKS

1 Yellowstone
2 Grand Teton
3 Rocky Mountain
4 Petrified Forest
5 Grand Canyon
6 Sequoia
7 Yosemite
8 Redwood
9 Crater Lake
10 Mount Rainier
11 Olympic
12 Cascades
13 Glacier

NATIONAL MONUMENTS

A Bad Lands
B Mount Rushmore
C Devils Tower
D Craters of the Moon
E Dinosaur
F Navajo
G Tonto
H Organ pipe Cactus
J Muir Woods

• Cities
⋯⋯ Routes
State Boundaries
┼ Grid Lines

KILOMETRES
0   400   800

Assignment A

1 Choose a route for Sally and David. There are 3 routes shown on the map.

  a) Choose a starting point: Sioux City, Kansas City or Dallas.

  b) List the cities, national parks and monuments they visit on your route.

  c) Give a 4 figure grid reference for each place visited on the route.

Sioux City is done for you as an example.

	NAME OF PLACE VISITED	NAME OF STATE	FOUR FIGURE GRID REFERENCE
1.	Starting point: Sioux City	South Dakota	(60,30)
2.			

2 Why do you think the route you chose is the most interesting?

3 Are Sally and David travelling from West to East or from East to West?

4 Work out a route from Seattle to San Diego visiting interesting places.

Personal Research A

Now choose three of the National Monuments and try to find out

a) What they look like.

b) Which President decided to create them.

These are Sally's photographs of four famous tourist places they visited on location. Below are David's descriptions of the same four places. The four places are called Muir Woods, the Bad Lands, Mount Rushmore and the Devils Tower.

A These hills are streaked in different colours like Liquorice All Sorts.

B A towering rock, 300 metres high, looking like solidified toothpaste.

C These giant redwood trees are the tallest living things in the world. They can grow 120 metres high, the height of a 33 storey building.

D Four presidents are carved out of the mountainside.

Personal Research B

Use an encyclopaedia and your library to find out more about these four places.

The Bad Lands Why were they so bad for early settlers?

Mount Rushmore What are the names of the 4 Presidents and why were they famous?

Assignment B

Read the descriptions and match them with the correct photograph.

PHOTO	DESCRIPTION A, B, C or D?	WHICH NATIONAL MONUMENT?
1		
2		
3		
4		

Devils Tower Used in which film by Stephen Spielberg? It was once hot volcanic lava. When it cooled cracks formed. Look for similar shaped rocks in the U.K. especially in Northern Ireland and West Scotland.

Giant Redwoods Search for some interesting facts about redwoods. Why do they grow so well on the Pacific Coast of the U.S.A.? Find out who John Muir was and why he is remembered in California. (Clue—conservation)

David liked Yellowstone best. Yellowstone was the first place in the world to be protected as a National Park. It is famous for its geysers which are columns of boiling water shooting high into the air.

David took this photo of a bear-proof trash can. A park ranger told him that about 40 visitors a year get clawed by bears. Rangers stun troublesome bears and take them in nets by helicopter to the wilder parts of the park.

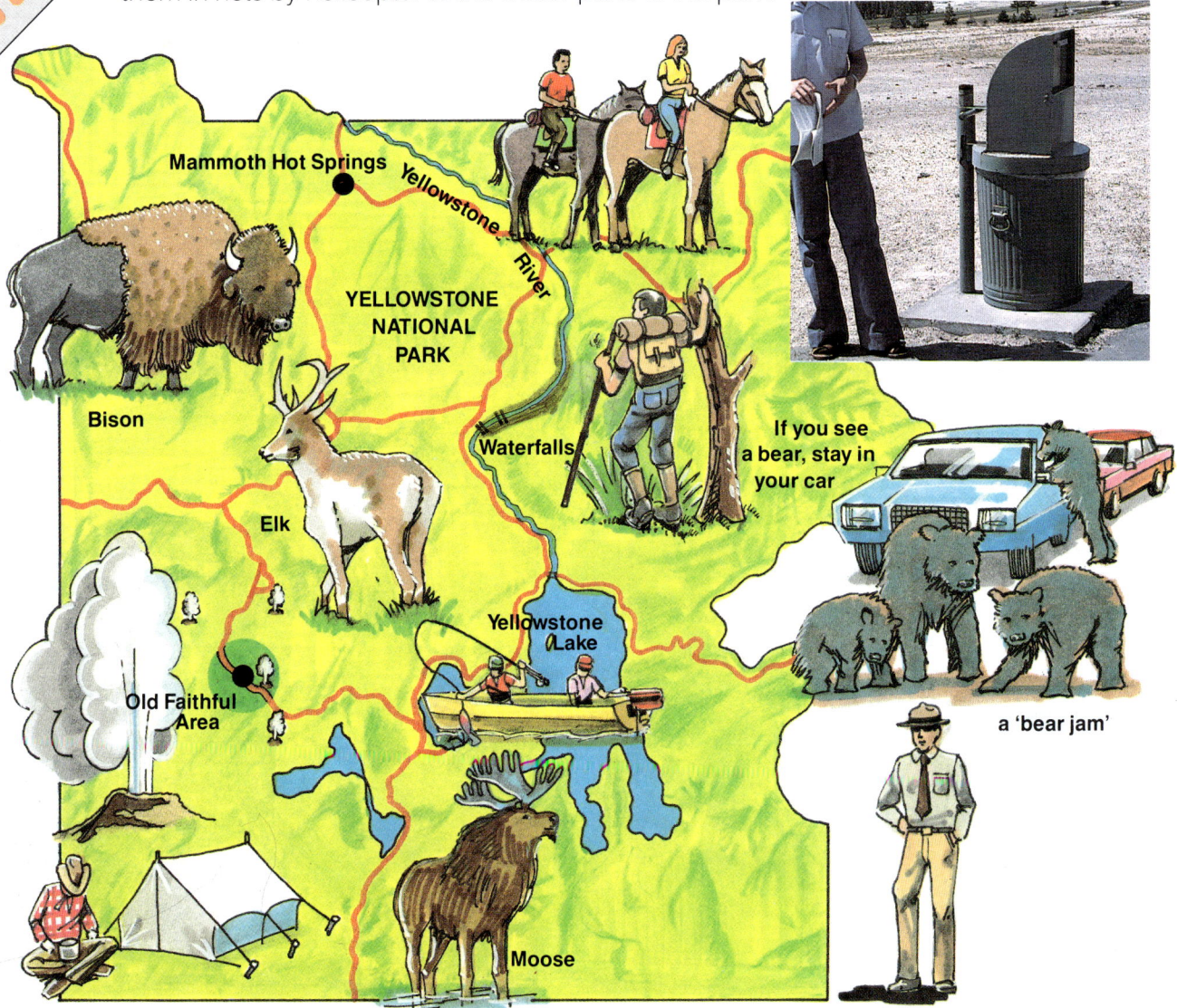

Mammoth Hot Springs

Yellowstone River

YELLOWSTONE NATIONAL PARK

Bison

Waterfalls

If you see a bear, stay in your car

Elk

Yellowstone Lake

a 'bear jam'

Old Faithful Area

Moose

Assignment A

1 Name four wild animals which live in Yellowstone National Park.

2 List four outdoor activities you can do in Yellowstone.

3 What is a 'bear jam' and why should you stay in your car?

4 What do we call a 'trash can'? Why have they been made bear proof?

5 Should the bears be allowed to roam free in the park? Discuss why they aren't shot or put into zoos.

6 Imagine you are camping in Yellowstone. A bear looks into your tent in the middle of the night. What happens next?

Sally liked riding on a rubber raft down the Colorado river through the Grand Canyon best. The stones carried by the river have slowly cut or **eroded** the huge valley.

The Colorado carries 500,000 tonnes of stones and mud every day and its valley is 1.9 kilometres deep. Sally discovered that the rocks near the top of the canyon are 225 million years old and dinosaur bones have been found in them.

Assignment B

Look at the photograph of the Colorado River running through the Grand Canyon. Imagine you are riding down this river on a raft. Describe what it is like. Some words to help: jagged rocks, white foaming water, current, whirlpool, rapids, spray.

Personal Research

Use your atlas to help fill in the gaps.

The source of the River Colorado is in the San Juan mountains in the State of _____. It passes through the States of _____ and _____ on its way to the sea. It ends in a sea called _____, part of the _____ Ocean.

THE FIRST AMERICANS

Snowshoes

California and Mid-mountain Indians

Indians living near the coast fished in the sea and hunted small animals. Those Indians living between the mountains found it more difficult to find food. Few crops grew and they often had to eat snakes and rats.

The main tribes were—Nez Perce, Shoshoni and Chumas.

Northwest Indians

They had plenty of food. The sea provided fish, seals and whales, with animals, nuts and berries from the forests. They lived in wooden houses and carved magnificent totem poles.

The main tribes were—Chinook, Tingit, Nootka.

Eastern Woodlands Indians

These Indians were farmers growing maize, beans and courgettes. They also fished in the sea, rivers and lakes. They were helpful to the first white settlers.

The main tribes were—Cherokee, Mohawk, Mohican and Seneca.

This map of North America tells us about where in the continent the Indians lived before white settlers arrived.

Assignment A

1   Copy and complete the key.
    The information you need is on the map and in the text.

2   Look at the five pictures.

   a) Which group of Indians carved totem poles?

      Why did Plains Indians not have them?

   b) Which group of Indians lived in Pueblo villages?

      Do you think this is an area of high or low rainfall?

      Explain your answer.

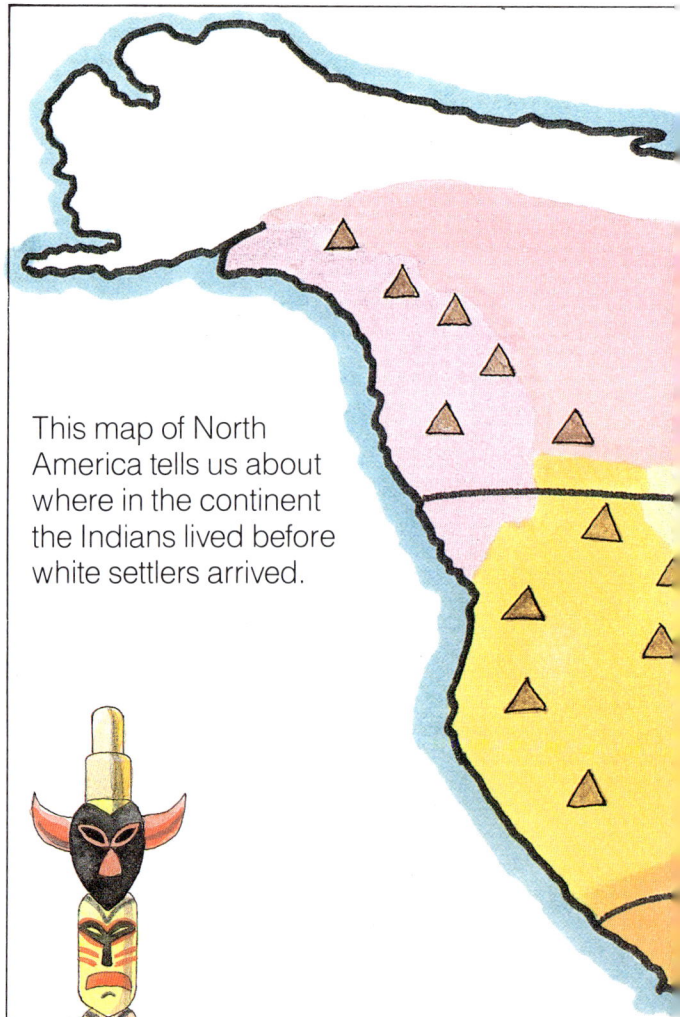
Totem pole

Pueblo house

Far North Indians

These Indians followed and hunted the elk, moose and caribous. Through the long winters they walked on snowshoes. Their tepees were covered with bark or animal skins.

The main tribes were—Cree, Chippewa, Ottawa.

Buffalo

Southwest Indians

These Indians often lived in large houses made of baked mud bricks. Whole villages could live in a single pueblo house. They made clay pots and beautiful silver jewellery. They grew crops near rivers.

The main tribes were—Apache, Navajo, Hopi, Zuni.

Plains Indians

Buffalo roamed the flat grassy plains and the Indians followed and hunted them. They ate the meat and used the skin and bones for their clothes, tools and homes. These Indians enjoyed fighting—they thought it was braver to touch an enemy and escape than to kill.

The main tribes were—Comanche, Sioux, Crow, Cheyenne, Pawnee.

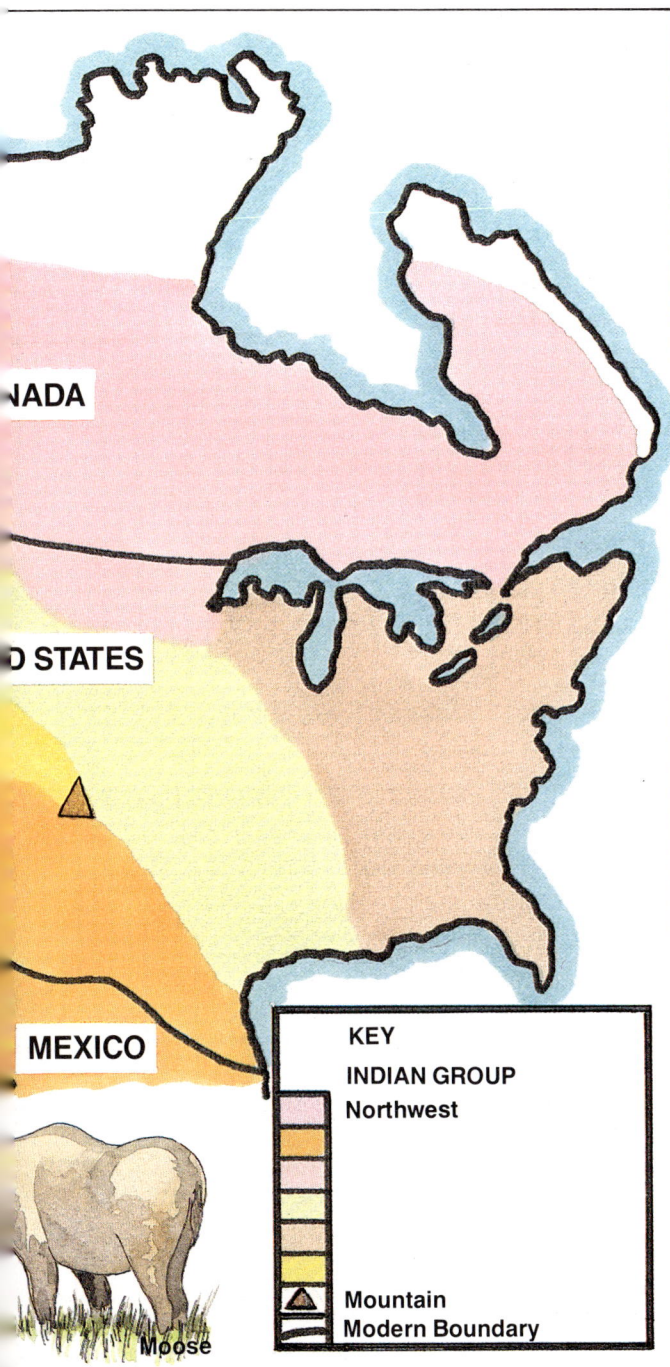

NADA

D STATES

MEXICO

KEY

INDIAN GROUP

Northwest

Mountain
Modern Boundary

Moose

Assignment B

a) Who depended on the buffalo?

b) Why did these people not build permanent homes?

c) Which group hunted the moose?

d) What use could the Indians have made of the antlers?

INDIANS: MYTH AND REALITY

The ways of life of the North American Indians were completely changed by the arrival of white settlers from Europe. Many of the Europeans wanted land to farm. As more Europeans arrived more land was needed—land that until then had been home for the Indians. At first **treaties** (agreements) were made with the Indians. The settlers broke the treaties when they wanted more land for farming or for mining.

Some land was reserved for Indians. These **reservations** were often on low quality land that the whites did not want. Many Plains Indians who enjoyed a nomadic life could not understand why anyone should want to stay in one place all the time. They did not have farming skills and so reservation land was not much use to them.

THIS SHOULD KEEP THE INDIANS OUT

BUT THIS TREATY SAYS THIS IS OUR LAND FOR EVER

WE WILL GIVE YOU HORSES AND GUNS FOR LAND

THIS WILL HELP US HUNT THE BUFFALO SO WE CAN SURVIVE

I DON'T CARE HOW LONG YOU'VE LIVED HERE. THIS IS MY LAND NOW

Assignment A

1 Look carefully at the pictures.

   How did the whites obtain land from the Indians?

2 Say why each was a poor deal for the Indians.

3 Imagine you were a white settler who had sailed from England to farm in America. Say how you would feel about the Indians.

4 Think about the different groups of North American Indians. Which group would find it easiest to live as farmers on reserved land?

   Which might find it impossible?
   Give reasons for your answers.

5 In school Indian children were not allowed to speak their own language. They had to become Christians and they had to have their hair cut short.
   Imagine that it happened to you. Write a story about what happened.

   What changes did you have to make?

   Describe your feelings and what you tried to do about it.

44

Assignment B

Have you seen a western on T.V. or at the cinema?

1 Draw a picture of a battle scene you can remember.

2 Who usually starts the fighting in the films?

3 Do you normally see women or children in the films? Are they white or Indian?

4 Do you think the stories they show are the true picture of what really happened?

5 Draw your idea of an Indian Chief in battle.

One step further A

1 Who wrote these comments, Indians or whites?

2 How do you know?

3 From information in the first passage, why do you think a reservation near mountains was offered to them?

4 Why would such an offer not be welcomed?

5 Why would going South lead to diseases?

6 Can you explain why people who had given up their guns should be killed?

One step further B

1 In most films we see young Indian men in battle. Discuss why old people like those above are not shown fighting in films.

What would make old people fight in this way?

2 If the films were made by the Indians would they tell the same stories in the same way? Explain your answer.

Now read comments made at the time of the wars.

We have been south and suffered a great deal there. Many have died of diseases which we have no name for. Our hearts looked and longed for this country where we were born. There are only a few of us left, and we only wanted a little ground, where we could live. I rode out and told the troops that we did not want to fight; we only wanted to go north, and if they would let us alone we would kill no one. My brother, Dull Knife, took one-half of the band and surrendered near Fort Robinson ... They gave up their guns and then the whites killed them all.

I have heard that you intend to settle us on a reservation near the mountains. I don't want to settle. I love to roam over the prairies. There I feel free and happy, but when we settle down we grow pale and die. I have laid aside my lance, bow, and shield. A long time ago this land belonged to our fathers; but when I go up the river I see camps of soldiers on its banks. These soldiers cut down my timber; they kill my buffalo; and when I see that, my heart feels like bursting; I feel sorry ... Has the white man become a child that he should recklessly kill and not eat? When the red men slay game, they do so that they may live and not starve.

This is Chica-ma-poo. The photograph was taken in 1903 when she was over 90 years old.

This is a real Indian chief, killed in battle. Compare it with your drawing of a chief.

North American Indians argue that some of their land should be given back to them. The Sioux Indians have asked for the Black Hills of Dakota because this area is sacred to them. Today the Black Hills are part of a National Forest in the U.S.A. which is popular with tourists. Now study the map of South Dakota.

Map

KEY

— Major Highways
△ Mountain

Natural Resources

- C Copper
- G Gold
- J Jasper
- L Lead
- S Silver
- T Tin
- U Uranium
- Timber

Redwater River

Beaver Creek

Crow Pk.
Spear Fish
Spearfish Pk.
C
Green Mt.
Iron Creek Lake
Lead City
G
L
Cheyenne Crossing
T
Elk Creek

BLACK

Silver City
Silver Pk.
S
Rapid Creek
Rapid City
Blue Lead Mt.

Crows Nest Butte

HILLS

Slate Creek

Bear Mt.
C
Battle Creek
J

NATIONAL

Custer
Custer State Park
French Creek
Wind Cave National Park

FOREST

Fall River
Custer River

Elk Mt.

Hot Springs

Flint Hill
U

KILOMETRES
0   10   20

Assignment A

1 What natural resources are found in the Black Hills which make the land valuable?

2 Why do the Indians value the land?

3 Which animal names appear on the map? (e.g. Beaver Creek)

One step further A

The names of places can provide clues to the past.

1 Complete the chart, one has been done for you.

PLACE NAME	POSSIBLE ORIGIN
French Creek	French settled here
Hot Springs	
Silver City	
Battle Creek	
Cheyenne Crossing	
Crow Peak	

2 Choose five other locations and add them to your chart. Compare your suggestions with those of your friends.

3 Why is timber valuable?

Personal Research

1 List the natural resources. Find out what they are used for and why they are valuable.

2 Identify on the map the locations which include the name Custer.

3 Who was Custer?

American Indians have found it difficult to obtain jobs in the past. These pictures show four Indians at work.

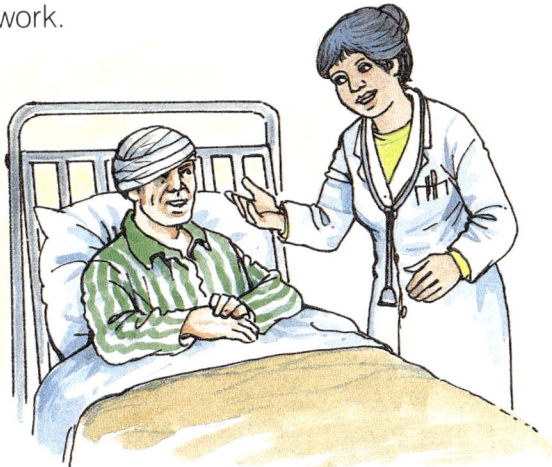

Assignment B

1 Complete the chart.

PICTURE	OCCUPATION	DOES THE JOB GROW SOMETHING, MAKE SOMETHING, OR PROVIDE A SERVICE?
A		
B		
C		
D		

2 Imagine you are an American Indian. Which job would you most like to do?

3 Describe how you would feel if you had to dress up in tribal costume for tourists every day.

4 Which of the four workers will only have a job during the holiday season?

One step further B

Study these facts about Indians today.

a) Their average pay is less than half that of White Americans.

b) Many have poor health and die young.

c) Many Indian children leave school before they finish their course.

d) More than half of American Indians are unemployed.

Discuss this situation with your friends. Why do you think things are so bad for Indians? Can you suggest ways of improving the situation?

TWO FARMS

This is Glen and Alice Scott at harvest time on their 200 hectare farm in Iowa, U.S.A. They grow maize and every bit of the crop is chopped up and stored in the silo. All the maize is fed to hogs kept indoors in warm buildings. The Scotts sell 2,500 hogs each year for bacon. Glen and Alice are worried because they owe the bank a lot of money. They borrowed money to buy more land and a new combine harvester.

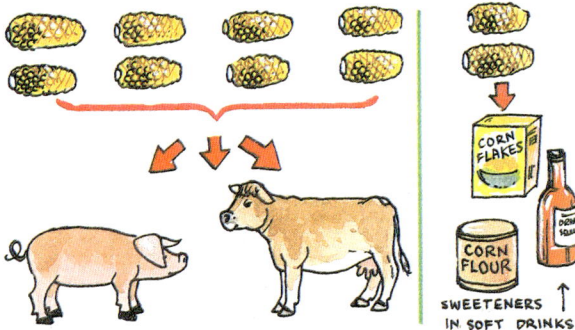

Hog finishing building

Silo

Propane gas tank   **Hog farrowing building**

Combine harvester

CORN FLAKES

CORN FLOUR

SWEETENERS IN SOFT DRINKS

Assignment A

1 How high does maize grow in Iowa? (Glen is 1.8 metres tall)

2 What name do we give to hogs?

3 Describe the shape of the fields.

4 What is the silo used for?

5 Why do the Scotts need so many machines?

6 Why is the gas tank there?

7 Why are the Scotts worried?

One step further A

1 What do you think about pigs never seeing daylight? Why do farmers do it? Is it right?

2 What would happen to the farm if they had no fuel for the machines?

This is Ghan and Shobha Dutt's farm in South India. They own three fields, but the fields are a long way apart. It takes ten minutes to walk from one field to the next. The three fields are very small, together they make two hectares. The Dutts grow enough grain, vegetables and fruit to feed themselves and their three children and they have a surplus to sell most years. This is their main field, their second is near a river and grows rice, the third is on dry ground and grows millet and maize. Rice, millet and maize are all **grain** or **cereal** crops. They have one bullock and one plough.

Assignment B

1 Why is farming more difficult if your fields are far apart?

2 Make a list of crops grown by the Dutts under three headings: a) grains, b) vegetables and c) tree crops.
Can we grow any of these in the U.K.?

3 How many different crops are grown by the Dutts?

4 List three differences between the Dutt's and the Scott's farms.

5 What similarities do they share as farmers?

One step further B

Study this picture

1 What is a vegetarian?

2 Who uses more of the world's food resources, a meat eater or a vegetarian?

3 Discuss with your friends and teacher the advantages and disadvantages of being a) a meat eater, b) a vegetarian.

RICE IN INDIA

Rice needs lots of water and heat to make it grow. It grows best in fields where the roots are covered in water and the top is in the hot sun. Rice is the main crop in many parts of India and is eaten mainly by the families that grow it. In some areas two crops of rice can be grown in the same field in one year. The rice is grown from seed for one month in nursery beds before being transplanted into the fields. The villagers all work together in everybody's fields in teams of ten for planting and for harvesting.

Which is best for rice farming, tractor or bullock?

What job is being done here?

Notice how everyone is working as a team at harvest time.

The bullocks do the threshing—to separate the grain from the husk.

Assignment A

1 Why are the rice seedlings grown in nurseries before planting out?

2 Why is it important to have earth banks around each small field?

3 How is the rice cut at harvest, and how is it threshed?

4 What do you think happens to the husks and straw?

One step further A

1 Imagine you are a villager at rice harvest time. Describe the work. Think about—sun, long days, sticky mud.

2 What advantages do the village people get by working together in teams?

Let's find out what sort of rock it is. The best way is to look at it through a handlens to find out if it is igneous or sedimentary or metamorphic.

Has it crystals, no layers, no fossils?

Yes - this is an igneous rock
No - think again

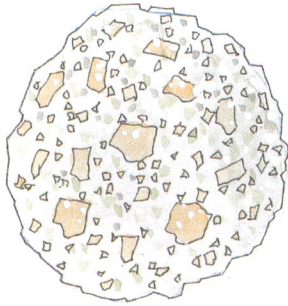

Is it in layers? Has it some bits of fossils?

Yes - this is a sedimentary rock
No - think again

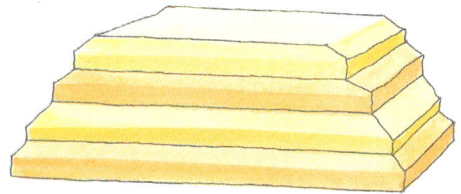

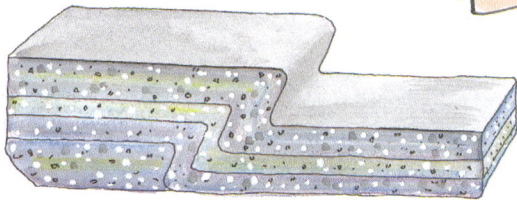

Limestone sedimentary rocks will fizz with a drop of vinegar.

Does it look as if it has been crushed?
Do some of the minerals in the rock look flattened or streaky?

Yes - this is a metamorphic rock
No - think again

Assignment B

Look at A, B and C. Decide which is sedimentary, which igneous and which metamorphic. Give reasons.

A

B

C

Personal Research

1   Dig a small hole in the school grounds with a trowel. Collect small stones and wash them. Classify them into the three types of rock. Watch out for things like brick or concrete!

2   Sort out a collection of beach pebbles collected on holiday.

3   Visit a local museum to look at their collection of rocks.

In America Sally found that people who collect rocks and fossils are called rockhounds. A **fossil** is the remains or trace of an animal or a plant, in a rock.

Assignment A

Match the fossils in 1, 2 and 3 with the pictures of the past, A, B and C.

What evidence have you to match fossil with picture?

One step further A

1 Coral fossils are common in old limestone rocks in many parts of Britain. Coral will only grow in very warm seas like the Caribbean. Complete this sentence: The evidence of coral in Britain suggests that a long time ago Britain was covered by ____ _____.

2 Draw a woolly mammoth. They lived in Britain one million years ago. What does its shaggy coat suggest about the weather at that time?

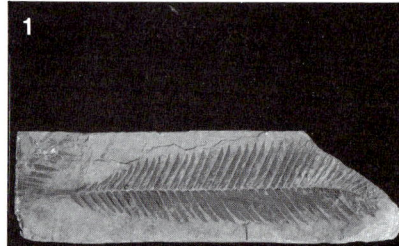
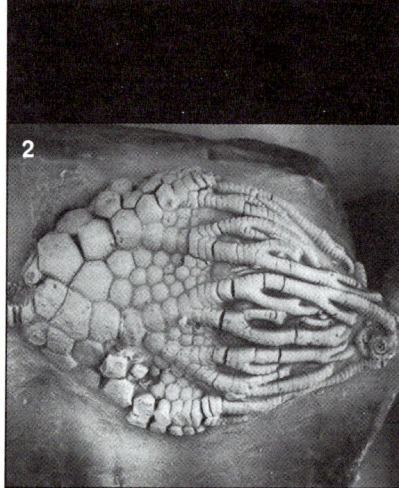

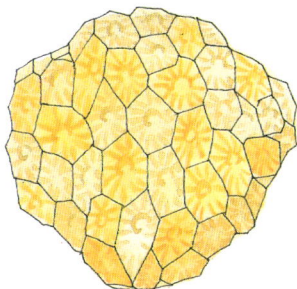

coral

mammoth

Personal Research

Discover why these two fossil hunters of the past became famous.
a) Mary Anning, a girl who lived in Lyme Regis, Dorset
b) Hugh Millar, a Stonemason, born in Cromarty, Scotland.

The first traces of life on earth are found in rocks about 3,000 million years old. These first fossils are simple creatures called algae. The earth formed about 4,600 million years ago. The diagram shows how life slowly developed from creatures in the sea to life on land and sea.

Assignment B

1 Did people live at the same time as dinosaurs?

2 How long ago is it that the first human-like apes lived?

3 For how many million years were dinosaurs living on earth?

   How does this compare to how long humans have lived on earth?

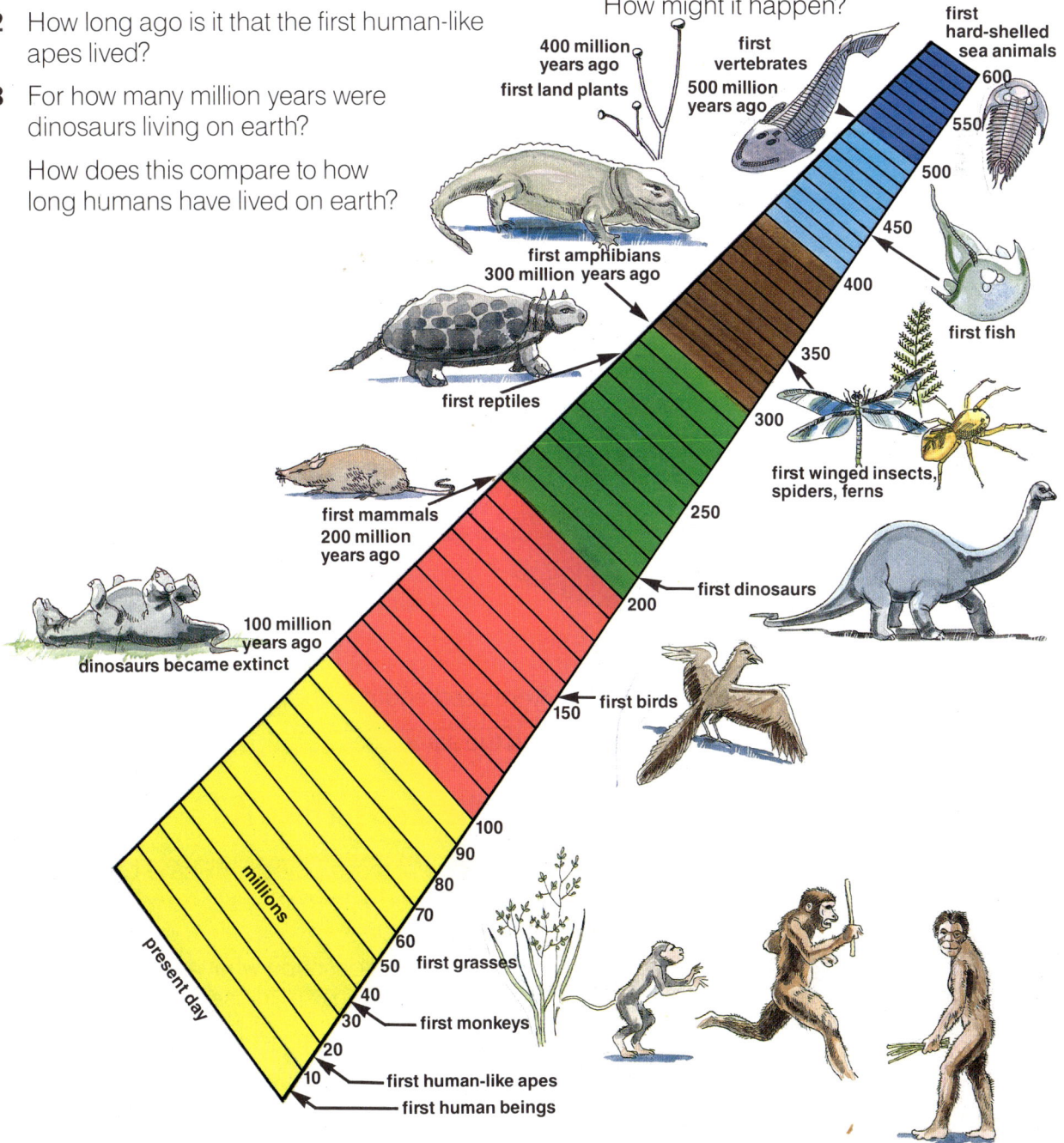

One step further B

1 Get a long piece of paper (a tough toilet roll will do) and mark or count 60 equal units to make a story of life diagram. Each unit is equal to 10 million years. Mark on your paper all the 'firsts' (first fish, first dinosaurs) on the correct ten million year unit.

2 What does extinct mean?
   Could the human race become extinct?
   How might it happen?

400 million years ago
first land plants

first vertebrates
500 million years ago

first hard-shelled sea animals

600

550

500

450

400

350

300

250

200

150

100

90

80

70

60

50

40

30

20

10

first amphibians
300 million years ago

first reptiles

first fish

first winged insects, spiders, ferns

first mammals
200 million years ago

first dinosaurs

100 million years ago
dinosaurs became extinct

first birds

millions

present day

first grasses

first monkeys

first human-like apes

first human beings

WATT NEXT?

Nearly everyone in Britain has electricity available in their home. However it is not that long ago when people had to manage without. Life was very different.

Past and Present

Assignment A

Six of the twelve pictures show modern electrical appliances. The other six show appliances which were used for the same purpose many years ago.

1 Match the old with the new.

Write a sentence for each pair matching a letter to a number.

2 Draw the pairs side by side.

List the differences you can see.

3 Now make a list of the similarities.

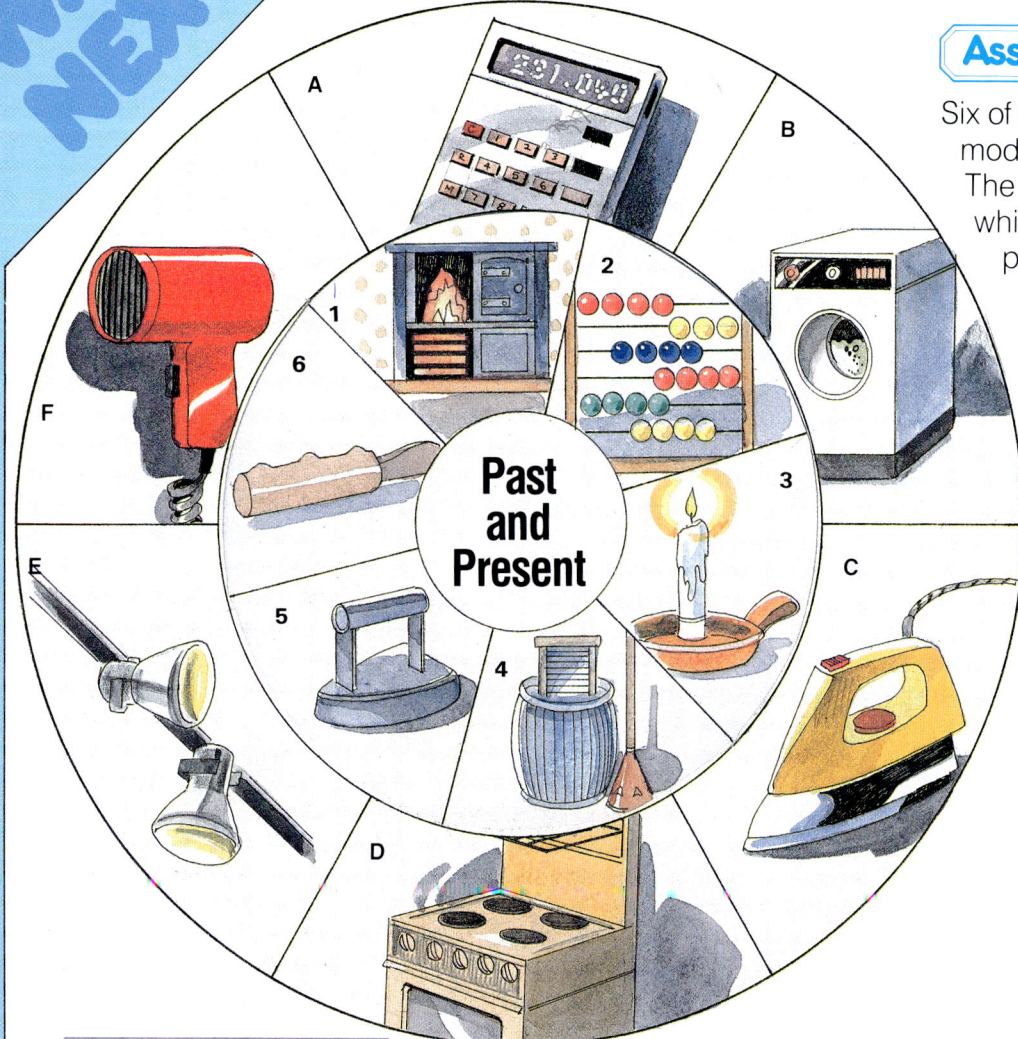

Personal Research

1 Find out the dates when the older appliances were used and how they worked.

2 Can you discover other old appliances which had the same uses as those in the picture?

One step further A

1 Look at these objects. All have been replaced with electrically-powered appliances.

Draw and describe what has replaced them. Are any still in use?

2 Imagine that from today the electricity supply stopped for ever.

Which appliance would you miss the most?

This is a section through one of the five new mines near Selby, North Yorkshire. All the coal from the five mines is carried to the surface by huge conveyor belts. The coal goes by train to electricity power stations. These trains, which never stop moving, are called *merry-go-rounds*.

Computers warn if any machine breaks down, or if dangerous gas forms. Machines do all the hard work: nobody touches the coal from the coalface to the electricity power station.

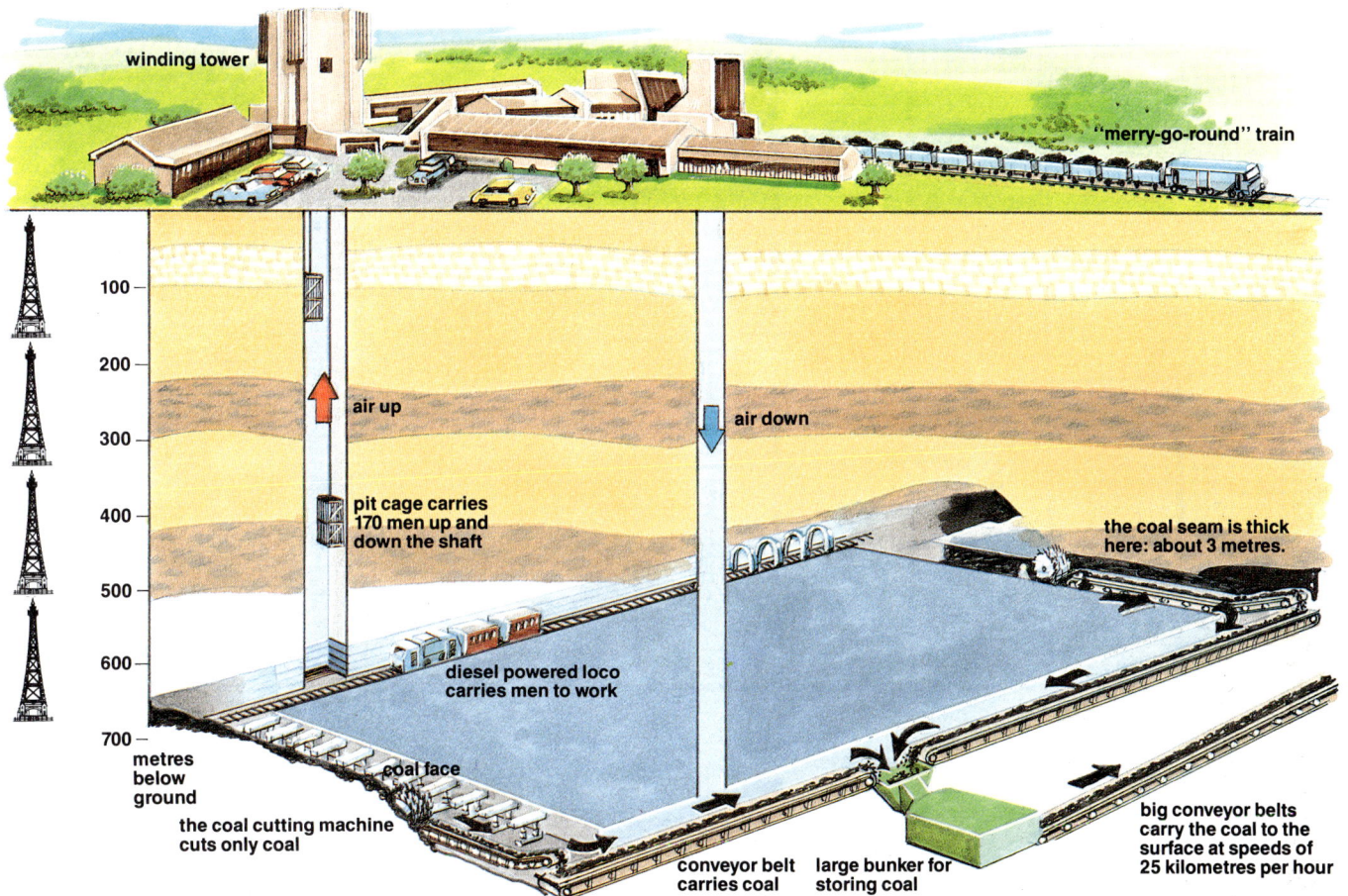

winding tower

"merry-go-round" train

100
200
300 — air up
400 — pit cage carries 170 men up and down the shaft
air down
500
600 — diesel powered loco carries men to work
700 —
metres below ground
coal face

the coal seam is thick here: about 3 metres.

the coal cutting machine cuts only coal

conveyor belt carries coal

large bunker for storing coal

big conveyor belts carry the coal to the surface at speeds of 25 kilometres per hour

Assignment B

Compare this new mine with the old mine of fifty years ago.

1 Which is deeper and which has the thicker coal seams?
2 How do miners travel to work today
   (a) overground?
   (b) underground?
3 Why are there no spoil heaps with the new mine?
4 Why is the coal train called a *merry-go-round*?

5 Each miner in one shift at Selby produces 12 tonnes of coal. This contrasts with only 2 tonnes in older mines. Why is it cheaper to get coal out at Selby?

Assignment C

Look at the photograph of the coal face.

1 Why do miners need a hard hat?
2 How is the coal cut?
3 How is the coal dust kept down? Why is this important?

The world's grain harvest.

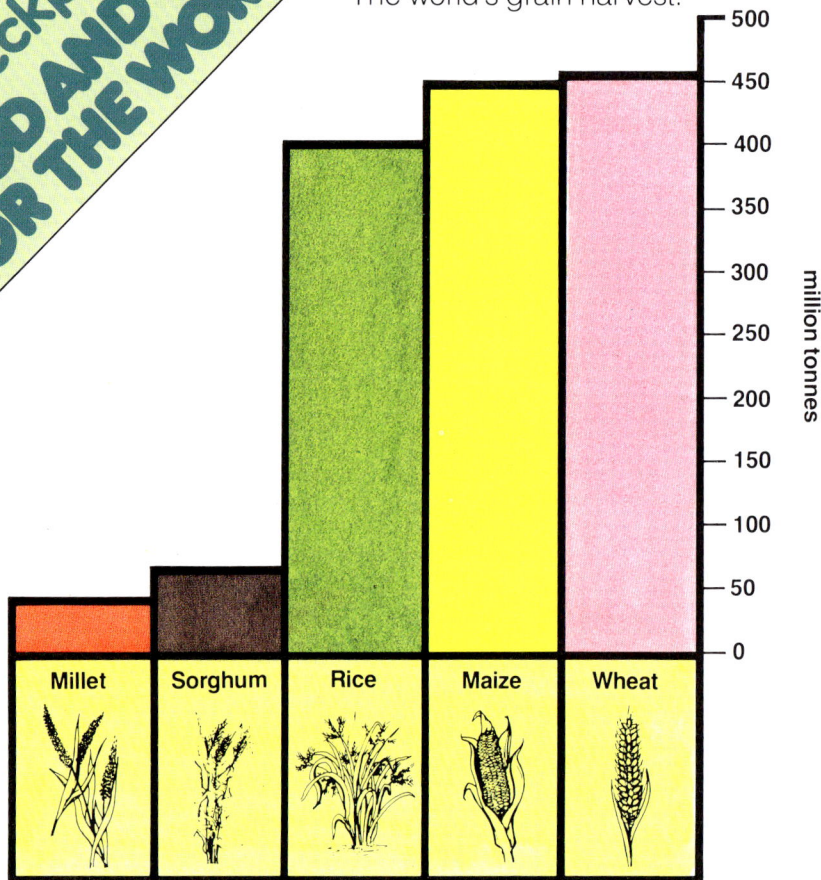

WHEAT

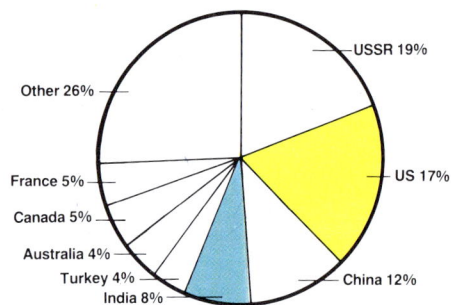

MAIZE

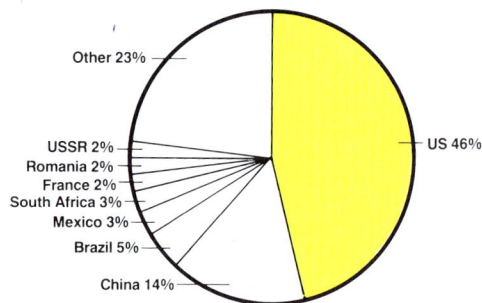

RICE

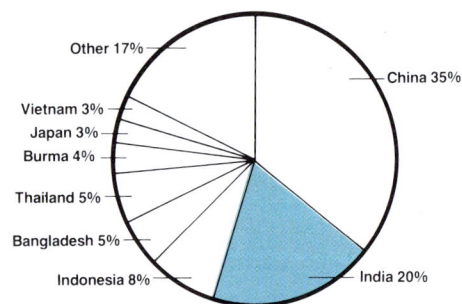

Assignment A

1 Which are the three most important grains in the world?

2 Complete the following:
The four countries which grow the most wheat are _____, _____, _____ and _____. The country which grows nearly half the world's maize is _____. The two most important countries for rice growing are _____ and _____. All the rice producing countries named on the graph are in the continent of _____.

3 Britain is not shown to be of world importance for growing grain but which of these cereal crops do we grow in Britain?

Personal Research

Using an atlas map look at world rainfall patterns. One of the three main grain crops grows best in dry, low rainfall areas.

Which one is it?

Another likes very wet conditions. Which one is it?

This graph shows the changes in fuel used by the world's people in the second half of the twentieth century.

FUEL FOR THE WORLD

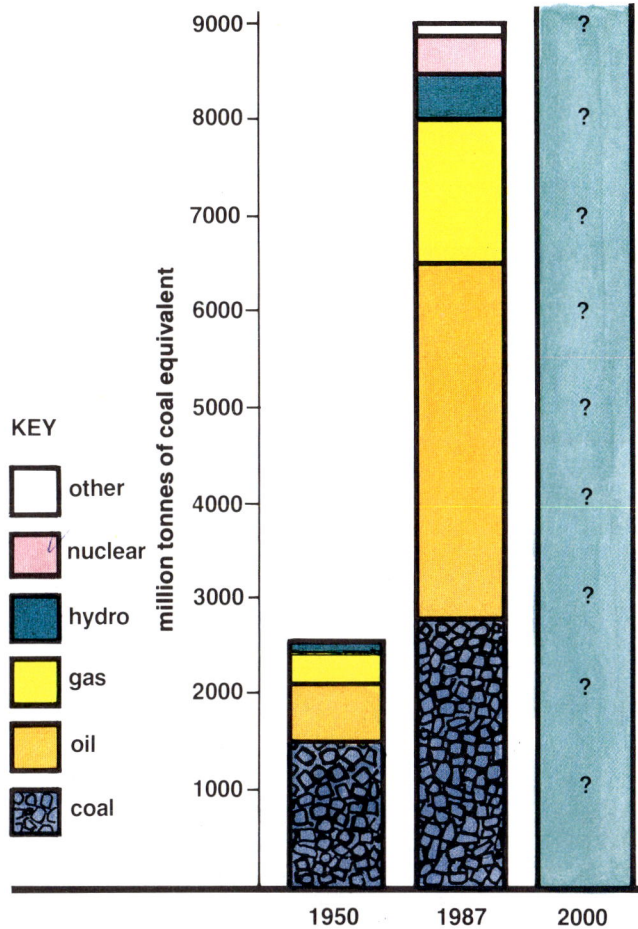

KEY
- □ other
- ▨ nuclear
- ▨ hydro
- ▨ gas
- ▨ oil
- ▨ coal

(y-axis) million tonnes of coal equivalent

9000
8000
7000
6000
5000
4000
3000
2000
1000

1950   1987   2000

Assignment B

1 What was the most important fuel in
a) 1950?   b) 1987?

2 Did the world use twice, three and a half times or five times as much fuel in 1987 compared with 1950?

3 Which do you think will be the four most important fuels in the year 2000?

4 Which fuel had not been tried out in 1950 but had become important by 1987?

One step further

Choose a suitable power unit for four different areas of India.

POWER UNITS	AREAS OF INDIA
A simple biogas (gas from manure) plant.	A big city near mountains with a lot of rain.
A hydro-electric power station.	A big city near a large coalfield.
A coal fired power station.	A village in a desert area with hot sun all year round.
Solar heating for cooking and heating.	A rural area with a lot of cattle.

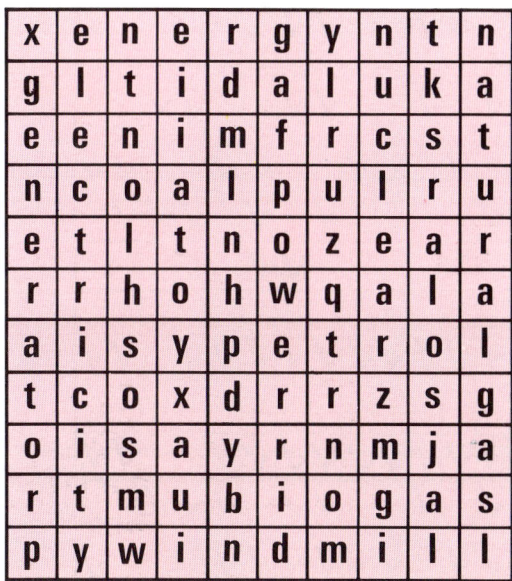

Wordsearch—There are 20 words in the wordsearch all about energy and fuels. Look horizontally, vertically and diagonally.

x	e	n	e	r	g	y	n	t	n
g	l	t	i	d	a	l	u	k	a
e	e	n	i	m	f	r	c	s	t
n	c	o	a	l	p	u	l	r	u
e	t	l	t	n	o	z	e	a	r
r	r	h	o	h	w	q	a	l	a
a	i	s	y	p	e	t	r	o	l
t	c	o	x	d	r	r	z	s	g
o	i	s	a	y	r	n	m	j	a
r	t	m	u	b	i	o	g	a	s
p	y	w	i	n	d	m	i	l	l

LOST PROPERTY   PETROL
GAS   OIL   DUNG
CANDLES   COAL

63

Skill/Concept Checklist

THEMES	SKILLS								ATTITUDES AND VALUES						CONCEPTS														
	Questioning	Research skills	Observing and recording	Processing	Communicating	Social skills	Physical skills		Empathy and World citizenship	Developing an enquiring mind	Open-mindedness to issues	Co-operation	Personal qualities		Function, process, force	Cause and effect	Movement and communications	Interdependence	Continuity/change	Self sufficiency	Conflict/concensus	Similarity/differences	Decision making	Conservation	Energy	Size/form/shape/symbols	Measurement etc.	Pattern	Values and beliefs
Homes	✓	✓	✓	✓	✓	✓	✓		✓	✓	✓	✓	✓		✓	✓	✓	✓		✓	✓	✓	✓	✓	✓		✓		
Power/Energy	✓	✓	✓	✓	✓	✓	✓			✓		✓	✓		✓	✓		✓		✓	✓	✓	✓	✓	✓	✓			
Physical	✓	✓	✓	✓	✓		✓			✓					✓			✓			✓			✓	✓		✓		
Mapping	✓	✓	✓	✓	✓	✓	✓			✓	✓	✓	✓		✓	✓	✓	✓		✓	✓					✓	✓	✓	
Leisure		✓	✓	✓	✓						✓					✓						✓	✓		✓				✓
Migration	✓	✓			✓	✓	✓		✓	✓	✓	✓	✓		✓	✓	✓	✓	✓	✓	✓	✓	✓	✓			✓	✓	✓
Land use			✓	✓	✓	✓				✓		✓				✓			✓	✓			✓		✓		✓		
Trade/Industry	✓	✓	✓		✓	✓				✓					✓		✓				✓		✓			✓	✓		
Shopping	✓	✓			✓				✓	✓			✓		✓	✓	✓		✓		✓				✓		✓		
Settlements	✓	✓			✓		✓		✓	✓					✓	✓	✓	✓	✓		✓	✓				✓	✓		
Urban/Rural	✓	✓	✓	✓	✓		✓		✓		✓	✓			✓	✓	✓	✓	✓		✓	✓	✓			✓	✓	✓	
Developed/Developing	✓				✓	✓			✓		✓		✓		✓	✓		✓	✓		✓	✓							✓
Transport/Communication		✓	✓	✓	✓				✓	✓					✓		✓				✓	✓			✓	✓			
Ecology	✓	✓	✓		✓	✓	✓		✓	✓	✓				✓	✓		✓		✓	✓		✓	✓			✓	✓	
Location					✓	✓	✓									✓			✓		✓		✓		✓	✓	✓		
Water		✓	✓	✓	✓	✓				✓		✓			✓	✓					✓	✓							
Food/Agriculture/Farms	✓	✓	✓	✓	✓				✓	✓	✓		✓		✓	✓	✓	✓	✓	✓	✓	✓	✓	✓	✓		✓	✓	
The Past	✓	✓	✓	✓	✓	✓			✓	✓	✓	✓	✓		✓	✓	✓	✓	✓	✓	✓	✓	✓	✓			✓	✓	
Weather		✓	✓	✓	✓	✓			✓			✓			✓	✓		✓			✓	✓			✓	✓	✓		
Distant Environments	✓	✓			✓	✓			✓	✓	✓				✓	✓	✓	✓		✓	✓	✓	✓	✓					✓

64